FAITH *on* FIRE

FUELING YOUR ENTHUSIASM

Merd:s,

The Lord bless + keep you !

LORI BECKER & SARA KEENER

Sara
10/27/07

ACW PRESS

ACW Press
Ozark, AL 36360

Faith on Fire
Copyright ©2005 Lori A. Becker and Sara A. Keener
All rights reserved

Cover Concept by Kathryn Lathers
Cover Design by Alpha Advertising
Interior Design by Pine Hill Graphics

Packaged by ACW Press
1200 HWY 231 South #273
Ozark, AL 36360
www.acwpress.com
The views expressed or implied in this work do not necessarily reflect those of ACW Press. Ultimate design, content, and editorial accuracy of this work is the responsibility of the author(s).

Library of Congress Cataloging-in-Publication Data
(Provided by Cassidy Cataloguing Services, Inc.)

Becker, Lori.

   Faith on fire : fueling your enthusiasm / Lori Becker & Sara Keener.
-- 1st ed. -- Ozark, AL : ACW Press, 2005.

   p. ; cm.

   Includes bibliographical references and index.
   ISBN: 1-932124-55-1

   1. Becker, Lori. 2. Keener, Sara. 3. Chaplains, Hospital--
Religious life. 4. Faith. 5. Spiritual life--Christianity. 6. Christian life.
7. Enthusiasm--Religious aspects--Christianity. I. Keener, Sara.
II. Title.

BV4501.3 .B43 2005
248.4--dc22   0504

Printed in the United States of America.

Dedication

This book,
created by God,
is dedicated to you, the reader.
The person that God has planned this moment for.
Your time to be
inspired,
encouraged
and
healed.

Table of Contents

Foreword

M any people have stories that began in their lives when they were little children; often they carry the pain of these experiences with them the rest of their lives. In such cases as these, they tend to repeat the same kind of shamed-based, abusive, destructive experiences in their lives and pass them on to their children. For generations these children will find someone who can help them live out the same pattern of behavior that their parent practiced. Indeed the scripture, "the sins of the father (and mother) are visited upon the children to the third and fourth generation (Ex. 20:5)," is manifested in a trans-generational cycle in the lives of those who continue the destructive behavior of their parent. Until somebody changes the pattern in their own life by speaking the truth, thus destroying the power of secrecy, each generation is at risk.

In this case, however, two women have teamed together, under the guidance of the Holy Spirit, to work through the devastation of their past horrors. In so doing, they are breaking the cycle in their own families and hoping to inspire others to do the same with the many stories in their lives. Lori and Sara did not know each other before. They were brought together in a program where they were both learning to become chaplains. As a part of the chaplaincy training, they had to tell their stories to their small group and their supervisor. As they worked and related together, they began to trust each other and share more of their stories with each other. They soon began feeling the love, power and grace of God bringing healing to each of them.

The clinical training in chaplaincy education is a process of hands-on pastoral care. Each of these women spent hundreds of hours listening and supporting individuals and family members through a myriad of cases of losses due to the death of loved ones, loss of little babies, health, self-esteem, and loss of relationships. As they listened to the stories of others, their own stories reared up in them and they had to find a way to work through their own pain, guilt, shame and disappointment. As they prayed for comfort, healing, and hope for the families to which they ministered, they experienced the same blessings for themselves. They credited their life-giving process to the openness of their peer group and the sensitivity of their fatherly like supervisor. He was a very spiritual and discerning person and developed a special bond between himself and each of these students. In time, there was an awakening inside of them that propelled them towards the idea of freedom.

They could not think of freedom for themselves without thinking of freedom for their siblings, their children, and legends of women who have suffered under the abusive hand of so many that they trusted and loved, anyone who had the power to steal the body, mind and spirit of another person and use it for their own satisfaction. Through the urging of the Holy Spirit, the authors found themselves willing to pool their resources of their own stories and work together to save themselves and their children. They heard themselves say that they needed to write their stories. They had both experienced journaling for years, but this guiding voice from within, was calling for more than private journaling. They were amazed at what they felt they were being called to do.

Through many days and nights of prayer they came to realize that they had to write a book. This heightened the anxiety to a fever pitch and made them reflect on how much they would have to give of themselves emotionally and physically; they thought of the cost to their families if they shared family secrets publicly. But, they also thought of the freedom that they could and would enjoy if they pushed ahead. Most of all, they thought of what could happen to their children and grandchildren if they failed to answer their call to write the book. They attended the Association for Clinical Pastoral Education (ACPE) Racial Ethnic Multicultural Invitational (REM) in Chicago as part of their chaplaincy training. They went a day earlier and one of their peers in their program who had lived in Chicago for some time helped these two small-town women experience the excitement, diversity, and energy of the big city.

Never before did these women feel so free and full of life. They ascended to the open view of the John Hancock building and caught sight of the city in all of its glory. They reflected, that this is what they were being called to experience. They could no longer settle for wading in the shadows of their painful past. The REM process was even more powerful for them on a spirit level. The music, speeches, workshops and sermons were beyond imagination, yet it was happening to them, with them and for them. They had never experienced such a spiritual high all around them. They were free to express themselves and enjoy affirmation from others of their freedom to be as they were and where they were. It was at this REM Invitational that they committed themselves to write the book that would change their lives and hopefully the lives of many others.

One might think that because they began on a high note and with a fast pace that everything would go smoothly in writing this book. Nothing could be further from the truth. It took a lot of prayer and working through one issue after another to get this task done. They experienced writer's block, rewrites, and disagreements about how to approach some of the chapters. They attended a writing conference and found some help for their process, but nothing freed them from the fear and anguish they felt in doing this task. They came to understand, fortunately, that this book was not theirs; it belonged to the Holy Spirit. Not until they were willing to give up complete ownership of the book and turn it over to the Lord, were they able to move ahead and complete this work.

The format of the book is that of each one telling her own story and then reflecting on the meaning and benefits of telling the story. Neither of these authors has been theologically trained, but they have learned to do theological reflection. They have intentionally not tried to teach theology in this book, but rather share where they are in their own theological journey. They do assert that for them it required a spiritual component to deal with the issues they were and are facing. They make no claim as to how anyone else should approach the issues in their own lives. Their hope is that in reading this book others will be stimulated to take the chance to move toward freedom in their own lives. ▬

Finally, it must be said that each of these women are married and have been long enough to have reared children. They plan to stay married to their present spouses, just so you know that this is not a male bashing thing. The authors have the support of their husbands in this venture and they know that all men or mothers are not abusive and destructive. They hope that men as well as women will read this book and find freedom for their own lives.

The cost to the authors for writing this book is not over; it will continue to exact payment for the rest of their lives. But, it will be a debt that they will gladly pay again and again as long as they can enjoy their freedom and they feel that they have helped others enjoy theirs.

Rev. Dr. Urias H. Beverly
Pastoral Midwife and author of *The Places You Go, Caring for Your Congregation Monday Through Saturday,* Published by, Abingdon Press

Our Psalm of Gratitude

How long, O LORD? Will you forget me forever?
How long will you hide your face from me?
How long must I wrestle with my thoughts
and every day have sorrow in my heart?
How long will my enemy triumph over me?

Look on me and answer, O LORD my God.
Give light to my eyes, or I will sleep in death;
my enemy will say, "I have overcome him,"
and my foes will rejoice when I fall.

But I trust in your unfailing love;
my heart rejoices in your salvation.
I will sing to the LORD,
For he has been good to me.
(Psalm 13)

Acknowledgments

Based on Psalm 13

We give thanks and praise to God for these special people:

God, though Urias, we have seen your Presence and heard your Voice. We lift our hearts in gratitude for our teacher, mentor and friend.

You have gifted Kath with the ability to give depth to our dancing spirits. Through her artistic talents she was able to illustrate our vision of celebration.

Lord, your love is reflected upon us in the hearts of those who have shared our journey to wholeness. Whit, Anne, Kathy, Nan, Diane and our faith communities are examples of the power of your Truth revealed through commitment to others.

We feel the strength and protection of your powerful Embrace as we are wrapped in the loving arms of our husbands, Duane and Les.

God, we thank you for the gift of our children and grandchildren, Jason, Krystina, Heather, Heidi, Brandon and Chaz. Looking into their eyes, we see hope for a better world.

We receive the blessings of the past through our parents,
Duane and Barb, Henry and Marian. Lord, may they continue to influence our lives as a mirror of your unfailing love.

We thank you for your gift of forgiveness.
We ask for the courage and wisdom to forgive those who
have contributed to our pain and struggle.
We believe your Love has created a radiant flower to bloom
in the deserts of our pasts.

We trust in your unfailing love;
our hearts rejoice in your salvation.
We will sing to the Lord,
For He has been good to us.
Our Faith is on Fire;
we live with enthusiasm for our God.

Introduction

*E*nthusiasm has taken on a new meaning for us. It has become more than an excitement or passion. In researching the original meaning of the word, we learned that it means "to be inspired, to be possessed by a god." We have become possessed by God, our creator and have felt the inspiration and ecstasy of the Holy Spirit within us.

Faith on Fire is a gathering of our stories, our experiences and our history. Some of which are extremely painful, while others are joyful and uplifting, yet all are a part of us. These stories make up who we are as a person of God. We have become persons of integrity and wholeness. Our lives are filled with enthusiasm. God has set our faith on fire.

Although our experiences are different, we each were carrying pain and scars from our pasts. Most of all we found that both of us have a deep hunger for God. We also share an unending commitment to helping others by following the call that God has placed in our hearts. It became obvious that God blessed our lives by arranging for us to be in the same hospital chaplain-training program, called Clinical Pastoral Education, (C.P.E.). The work that God had planned for us was unknown, until now. This book is the first fruit of God's vision for us. It is the next step in our journey with God.

Our education through C.P.E. provided not only the necessary tools to give pastoral care to others, but it also became the foundation for the spiritual growth we have achieved. The most important thing we learned in our training was that to be totally present with someone going through a difficult time, we need to be aware of the pain and sufferings from our own past.

We believe that God gave us a community of our peers to support, encourage and challenge us to look within ourselves and learn from the experiences in our lives. This is what C.P.E. provided for us. It was our chance to grow into our relationships with ourselves and with God. Now that our foundation is firm, it is time for us to share what we have learned with others.

We have been inspired by God to look at our issues again, feel the pain that they caused and then write our stories. This book does not belong to us. It belongs to God. Our journey through the chapters has strengthened us in ways that we did not expect. We are not the same two women that began writing this book. Our prayer is that you will be filled with the Spirit of Holy Fire as we were and your life will also be changed forever.

In the days that followed the conception of this book, God placed a burden on our hearts to reach out and help others through our words. Even though we have dramatically changed, the focus that we began with remains the same;

We pray that our stories will empower our daughters and sisters, sons and brothers, both in blood and spirit with the wisdom, knowledge and enthusiasm to realize that we can leave behind the experiences we've had that held us bound like heavy chains, open our gift from God and become a whole person surrounded by the Glory of God.

In order to keep our hearts on this focus, God has given us these Truths to live by and to share with others:

God is present within us and around us.

God reveals the truth through our struggles.

God calls us to a life of service.

God's voice is heard through all creation.

God delights in us.

God sees treasure in every person.

God's community is the fuel of divine energy.

God desires relationship with us.

God's love is revealed through others.

God promises to fulfill our needs.

God listens to our hearts.

God is the essence of life.

God's Truths are eternal.

We welcome you to join us as we sit on God's lap and listen to the breath of the Holy Spirit. As you listen to our stories, we invite you to be open to exploring how God's Truths are present in your life.

Spiritual Reflection

Through our learning during C.P.E we have come to deeply appreciate spiritual reflection. Each experience or event in our lives brings a richness of insight if we take time to reflect on what has happened. At the end of each chapter of *Faith on Fire*, you will find our reflections on the stories we've shared. Reflection is a way of bringing closure, of tying up loose ends and learning more about our inner selves. We hope that you will enjoy the treasures we have found through our reflections and that they will encourage you on your journey to becoming a person of enthusiasm.

CHAPTER ONE

Pentecost
The Spirit of Holy Fire

The afternoon soaps were playing on the television and Annie was curled up on the couch, wrapped in a blanket, engrossed in the program. Even though it was February in Michigan, the sun shone brightly through the windows. The beautiful rays warmed the room, yet for Annie, life felt cold and bleak. During a commercial she looked around. Her home had become cluttered and disorganized. There were Christmas decorations still piled in the corner waiting to be put away. The holidays had come and gone. It was almost Valentine's Day and Annie had not found the energy to move forward. Her life had lost meaning and purpose from the moment the doctor told her she had breast cancer.

Things were so different just six months ago. Life was busy, there was so much to do. Her days were filled with activity, going to work, cooking meals, doing the laundry and being mom to her three teenagers. Her identity as a mother extended into her working world also. She was the one to bake cookies, listen to troubles, help with extra work. There seemed to be little time for herself, but this was all that she knew.

Suddenly she lost control of her life. Now her world was filled with doctor appointments, tests and chemo. The strength in her body had disappeared. She was so sick from the treatments and missed so many days of work that she lost her job. She didn't want to burden her children with her illness so she carried the load herself. The kids were afraid and didn't understand what it was happening to her, so they distanced themselves. The once busy house had become her tomb. The people that she thought were her friends don't call. She felt abandoned and alone.

The doctors assured Annie that her surgery and treatments have been successful, but she believes that not only did the cancer rob her of her breast, it also stole her soul and identity. She is engulfed by the emptiness and meaninglessness of her life. To escape the many questions going through her mind she transports herself into the fantasy world of the soap operas. However, the TV is only a short-term tranquilizer for her pain.

When the program ended, her questions returned. She asked herself, "If there is a God, why does my life feel like hell?" She threw off the blanket and went to the refrigerator searching for something that would satisfy her hunger. "Nothing looks good in here." She slammed the door and felt surrounded by hopelessness and fear that she will never feel complete again. She walked past the sink filled with dirty dishes and said, "I can't believe I've let everything become such a mess."

The mess is reflected not only in a disorganized home, but in her life. Annie thought if only she had a friend like the people on the soaps had, then her life would somehow be tolerable. Someone would be available to lean on and she wouldn't be alone. She had no idea where to turn or who to ask for help. Annie thought back to some of the dark days of chemotherapy and remembered a woman who came and sat with her. Annie didn't remember much of what she had said, but she knew she had felt comforted because this woman cared about her. Recalling this, Annie felt a ray of hope that the woman might remember her. This hope gave her the courage she needed to call the treatment center to ask if anyone knew who the person was that had visited her.

Fortunately, the receptionist that answered the phone knew that a chaplain visited the center twice a week. She then transferred Annie's call to the pastoral care department of the hospital. Annie received compassion and care from the secretary who promised to have the chaplain return her call. As she hung up the phone, she questioned herself; "Why did I do that? Nobody will remember me. Who's going to care about my problems, anyway?" Annie looked at herself in the mirror. Because of the treatments she had lost her hair and gained weight. Who was the woman in the baggy T-shirt looking back at her? "Will I ever feel like a woman again?" she asked the image in the mirror.

She turned away from the mirror and yelled at God, "What did I do to deserve this? Life has been hard enough for me as a single parent and now this! This is not fair!" She fell into her bed and cried herself to sleep. When the kids came home, they found their Mom sleeping, again. As they made their own dinner, they wondered if their lives would ever be the way it used to be.

The next morning the ringing of the phone awakened Annie. She yelled for the kids to answer, not realizing they had already left for the day. As the phone continued to ring, she picked it up in frustration. A woman's voice gently replied, "Good morning. This is Chaplain Naomi. I'm returning your call. How can I help you?"

Annie listened in bewilderment and amazement. Someone had returned her call. She didn't know what to say, but muttered, "I don't know if you can help me or not. I remember someone sitting with me when I had chemo. Could that have been you?" Annie could not believe what she was hearing as Naomi replied, "Yes, it probably was, I'm assigned to the treatment center. How have things been going for you?"

Tears of gratefulness filled Annie's eyes as she realized that someone did care about her. "Thank you so much for calling me, I've been so alone. I feel like I'm losing my grip on life. I got so sick with the treatments, lost my job, can't be a mother and hate what I see when I look in the mirror." Annie choked back a sob.

Naomi heard the despair in Annie's voice. Her life had also been filled with pain, so she was able to empathize with Annie. Naomi's experience had taught her that Annie needed to be surrounded by hopeful, supportive people as she had been in her darkest hours. Others who would understand her struggle. "Annie, I can hear in your voice that this has been a painful time for you. Can you tell me more about your last couple of weeks?"

Annie explained to Naomi that the doctor's reports and test results were good. She talked about how things have changed and her feeling of having lost control. "The doctors tell me I can return to a normal life, but I can't. How can anything be normal after this?"

Naomi asked, "Have any of your doctors encouraged you to attend a cancer support group?"

"They may have," Annie said, "but I don't remember. It was such a confusing time."

Naomi told her about a group that met at the treatment center every week and offered to go with Annie the first time. Annie was hesitant, but willing to try, because she somehow felt that she could trust Naomi.

It has been several months since Annie began attending the support group. Through the relationships she has developed, she has found the friendship she had longed for. Annie has learned from listening to other's stories that each person in the group is a survivor, and she has begun to think of herself as one, too. She surrounded herself with community and was gifted with hope. With a new spirit and purpose she has learned that through her struggles, she has become a woman of courage. Someone with the courage to look at her life with different eyes. Each day is a gift rather than a burden. She has come to believe that God was present with her through Naomi on one of her darkest days. God has proven to Annie that she can trust in His promise that He will always be present with her. In truth, Annie has experienced her Pentecost, for God's Spirit now lives within her. She has found an enthusiasm for life that she had never known before. Annie's new life has begun.

Holy Fire Reflections

A group of people were gathered together waiting for what their teacher had promised would come. Their world had been turned upside down by his death. They lost their purpose, direction and meaning for life. They felt alone and abandoned and wondered what was ahead for them. The only sense of security was to stay together in the room, because they feared that those outside, who didn't understand, would harm them. So they waited.

In the midst of their despair they heard a strong wind blow through the house with a roar. They became more frightened when they saw what looked to be tongues of fire falling down upon them. Everything seemed to be out of control, but yet, they began to feel an energy that consumed their whole being. This energy was a fervent warmth that produced a glow within each of them. In the midst of this power their fears evaporated. They were filled with an enthusiasm to share with others all that they believed. This is the story of Jesus' disciples after His death and resurrection. The day was Pentecost. The Spirit of Holy Fire had filled their hearts with God's love just as Jesus had promised.

When difficult times come into our lives we may feel lost, frightened, abandoned and sad, just as Annie and Jesus' followers did. God asks us to watch and wait for the Spirit to provide comfort and solidarity by urging us to reach out to others. The connections that we make form a community of hope for us, which fuels our enthusiasm for life. The dark days of despair and hopelessness are replaced with a sense of belonging and purpose. And, we feel an eagerness to tell everyone all that we believe. This is our Pentecost.

Fuel for your journey

1. Does Annie's story seem familiar to you?

2. What feelings do you have in common with Annie?

3. Is there a Naomi in your life that you can reach out to?

4. Are you ready for your Pentecost?

CHAPTER TWO

Fear

The Paralyzer

Fear is like a mangy alley cat slinking through the dark corridors of our mind. It is the monster under the bed or the ghost in the closet. Fear is sinister and holds us bondage to secrets hiding deep within our beings. Fear confines us to the small perimeters of the box we have built around ourselves. Fear incapacitates and paralyzes our body, mind and spirit.

Sara

First Grade Fears

Fear invaded my life around the age of five. Since my twin brothers and I were close in age I never did anything alone until I began first grade. Climbing into the big yellow school bus alone was a very frightening experience. Tall kids I did not know were sitting on the seats, high school students, strangers in my small world. At this point my world consisted of family and church friends. I had never been to a grocery store because Mother ordered our groceries over the phone and the delivery-man brought them to our home. They only time we went shopping was for new shoes, because everything else was ordered through the catalogue.

My first day of school was very traumatic. I can only imagine what was going through my five-year-old mind. I got off the school bus and ran to the house wanting to tell Mommy about my first day of school. Grandma told me that Mommy was in the hospital and I had a new baby sister, but that was not important to me. I wanted the love and security of Mommy's arms and she was gone. I had left for school alone and came home feeling abandoned.

Even though school consisted of one room with both first and second grade it was a scary place. My teacher, Mrs. Landis, helped this frightened little girl to feel safe. One morning I came into the building only to find a strange woman behind the teacher's desk. One of her hands was deformed and I went to the coat closet and cried. Walter, a second-grade boy with red hair, came and attempted to comfort me.

Since I was the firstborn in the family, my parents wanted to do everything perfect. Mommy chose not to read or tell her children anything but true stories. In school, Mrs. Landis read to us the story of "Little Red Riding Hood." For a child who knew only stories that truly happened, the world of fairy tales was frightening. I thought the story was true and a wolf would come to eat my grandma. If he did not eat Grandma, I was sure the big, bad wolf was following me everywhere I went.

Fear of making mistakes has been troublesome for me to work through. Even in first grade I remember sitting at my desk, crying because I could not make a perfect capital S. The curvy letter had too many twists and turns for my small hands to maneuver. As a nurse in training I can still see the tip of the Foley catheter quivering as I attempted for the first time to catheterize a patient. Even though I worked for seven years in a pediatrician's office, every time I gave the babies their immunizations I feared I might make a mistake. Mistakes made at home as a child did not always mean punishment, but rather, a lack of approval. Approval from those in authority determined my self worth.

Fearful Games

At times, my fear played unrealistic games with my mind. When my sister was born, my mother needed some rest and I went with my grandparents to visit some of their friends. We had been invited for dinner and my grandparents told me that a woman would be present who had mental disabilities. In their attempt to explain this in simple terms, they apparently said that she does not have all her brains. We had peas at the meal and I had always eaten them with a thin cream sauce or a bit of milk. I was served the peas alone and I could not manage to eat them because I was sure the peas were some of the woman's brains. I had a pit in the bottom of my stomach and never wanted to go to that home again.

I remember as a twelve-year-old being left in charge of my six younger siblings when my parents went to a meeting. I almost freaked out, imagining all that could occur when I was responsible. What would happen if Dad and Mom died and I was left with all my brothers and sisters? I was responsible for their well being and that was frightening.

Fear was a visible enemy of mine as a young teenager. We had a visiting minister preach at our church and he spoke on 1 John 4:18,

> *"There is no fear in love. But perfect love drives out fear…"*

I do not remember what he said but I was so impressed with the fact that love drives out fear that I posted the verse on my bulletin board in my bedroom. I wondered if it was God's perfect love that would drive out the fear or if my own love had to be perfect before fear would be driven out of my life.

I feared new experiences in high school. I often felt inadequate; as a result it became very comfortable to crawl into the small box of safety I had built around myself. A year after graduating from high school I had a desire to attend college. I did not like math in school so I had taken the easier business math classes. Realizing I needed algebra if I was to pass the entrance exams for college, I enrolled in a correspondence course for algebra. After studying the textbook for several weeks, I came to the conclusion it was too difficult an undertaking. Often I looked at the Wheaton College catalogue that I received in the mail, but my fear of failure paralyzed me. I do not know what became of the textbook, but with the fear of algebra, my dream of going to college ended. I decided to attend a bible school that did not require an entrance exam. Many dreams are lost as a result of fear!

A Mother's Fear

When Heidi, our daughter, became of college age I thought I could live out my dreams through her. That belief almost ruined the relationship I had with my daughter. She was a good student and had plans to attend college with almost a full scholarship. I was elated with her decision. But, Heidi's plans changed and the monster of fear began residing under my bed. Three days after she graduated from high school, Heidi packed all her belongings into her car and drove over six hundred miles to be with the young man she loved, a former school friend, with whom she became reacquainted when we returned to Pennsylvania at Christmas to visit with family. After living with her grandparents for three months she saved enough money for a security deposit on an apartment. About twice a month Heidi and I would attempt to have a conversation over the phone. It was usually short and to the point because neither of us knew what to say. I feared I had lost my daughter.

Later that summer when I visited her, I burst into tears. I could hardly control myself. I loved her so much. How could things have gone so wrong? I had dreams of my daughter going to college and becoming the person I wished I could have been. How could God be allowing this to happen to my child? Brandon's mother had helped her to decorate and provided most of the furniture for her cute little apartment. I felt alienated. Another woman had taken my place.

My heart was broken and the fear monster paralyzed me! But, God provided an answer! I became part of a Moms In Touch prayer group. Two other moms and I chose to meet weekly for one hour to pray for our young adult children. Together, we spent time praising God for who He is, confessing our sins silently to the Lord, thanking Him for the prayers He had answered and then interceding on behalf of our children. Each week we prayed a scripture, inserting our child's name in God's promise. Here was a place to voice my fears. I found faith that God loved my daughter more than I did. He would take care of her. Some weeks I was able to give my child to God and other times I would carry the pain for Heidi in my heart.

There were times I cried for my daughter and also for myself. I felt I was a failure as a mother. Today, I wonder why I felt like a failure. Heidi was my daughter; my responsibility, and I feared I had failed her. It was much like fearing my responsibility of watching my siblings when I was twelve.

In September, Heidi and Brandon chose to get married and I was ready to accept their decision. Because my own marriage had brought much pain into my life I feared for Heidi.

Since I keep my feelings bottled up inside of me, my body ends up paying the price. Soon after the wedding I became so ill that I took leave of my nursing position. A weakness came over my body so that I hardly had enough energy to breathe. I was sent to one specialist after another seeking an answer to my health problem. Nine months later I had surgery for an adenoma that was on one of my parathyroid glands. During this time, Heidi called and told us they were expecting a baby in December. I wanted to be happy for them. But fear paralyzed me! I thought, "A baby, when they are so young, inexperienced and immature." In the midst of the dark cloud of fear, Chaz, our first grandchild brought a ray of sunshine.

Sometimes when Heidi and I would talk on the phone, I would ask if they had found a church. The answer was no, and soon I stopped asking. I was still meeting with my Moms In Touch prayer group. Then one day, Heidi told me they had gone to church and they thought it was one they would begin attending on a regular basis. I rejoiced with that bit of good news. Several weeks later Heidi said Brandon was a new man. He had answered God's call to become a Christian.

In January 2002, Heidi and Brandon asked that we be present when they were baptized in water as a symbol of their faith in Jesus. What a glorious evening that was when we heard Brandon give his testimony of how God had called him. Afterward, I went to Heidi and asked her to forgive me for all the cruel things I had said about Brandon. As we held each other and cried, she replied that she had forgiven me a long time ago. Later I found Brandon, placed my hands on his shoulders, looked into his face and told him I was so very proud of him. I love him and believe he is a true man of God.

I realize now that I handled my fear by turning to God in prayer. What I could not fix or resolve I gave to God. At times I became angry with God for not answering my prayer like I thought He should or in the time frame that I wanted. When my faith became weak, others were speaking words of assurance to me. In the midst of my frailties and struggles God chose to answer my prayers. God does not seek perfection, rather an open and honest heart.

Another situation in my life that caused fear to raise its ugly head was when our daughter Heather was diagnosed with a language disability. The feeling of fear either causes me to fight or give flight. In Heather's case it caused me to fight. When Heather was three she still could not speak so others could understand her. Because speech problems ran in the family I sought help. It was through early testing that we learned Heather had difficulty processing. As she got older this affected her ability to read, spell and think through math story problems. I will always be grateful to the child psychologist who told me that the earlier and more intense the therapy, the greater the opportunity for benefit. I was fighting for my daughter because I did not want her to live with poor self-esteem. I taught her that she could do most anything she put her mind to. If that did not work then she would learn to compensate. This journey has not been an easy one for Heather or myself. I feel a mother's pain when I see her struggle with areas that come easily for others. It is not fair that my child should have to struggle with reading and spelling difficulties.

When Heather was entering tenth grade she wanted to be in the regular English class. She wanted a particular teacher because she believed he could prepare her for college level writing. Within the first week, the teacher told her she was not smart enough to be in his class. This comment put me in the fight mode. I arranged for a conference to review Heather's Individual Education Plan, which involved the English teacher. That week at the Moms In Touch group I asked that they pray God would pave the way for me to present my concerns and that I would be heard. God provided beyond what I could have even imagined. Before the meeting was over the teacher had arranged that she would have the help of the special education teacher every day for the English assignments and also be able to be in his class. Heather worked very hard that year and received an A in the class. I learned that even though I was fearful, I could stand firm and fight for what I thought was right for my daughter.

My Fear-Filled Marriage

The ghost of fear almost destroyed my marriage. As I mentioned earlier, new experiences often brought fear into my heart. I had a fear of the sexual experience because it was new for me. Because my husband, Les, was physically aggressive when we were dating I was very nervous and frightened on our wedding night. I had saved myself for my husband, but my anxiety and fears became uncontrollable. Our first night together was a disaster. I was in tears and my fear of sex mushroomed.

As a child I was taught that if you did not have anything good to say about someone it was best not to say anything. This caused much trouble with my husband. I was not happy with our marriage situation, but I never shared any of these feelings with him because they were "bad" feelings. Instead of fighting for my marriage I ran away emotionally. Fear, the mangy alley cat, was slinking through the dark corridors of my mind.

It was before Christmas and we were deciding where to put the tree. Heidi and I wanted it in front of the window and Les thought it would be best in the corner of the room. He did not want to move the sofa and I saw no problem with moving it. He commented that nobody cared that his back hurt and I replied that if his back hurt that much he should go to bed. He went to bed and Heidi and I rearranged the room. Later that evening the floodgates burst open and I told Les that if he did not consent to long-term counseling the girls and I would leave. That comment hit him like a bombshell because he had no idea I was feeling that distraught. He wanted to talk about our relationship, but I refused because fear paralyzed me!

When I was with our therapists I felt safe enough to spill out all the pain I had kept inside. I had reason to fear my husband, but I chose to begin to fight for my marriage. Physical closeness was one of my fears so I chose to meet it head on. When we were in bed I moved over against the strong muscular body of my husband. I allowed him to hold me and together we wept tears of joy, knowing that I had taken the first step in facing my fear.

Lori

Fear Has Always Been There

Fear has always been part of my life. It has been the fuel that drove my self-esteem into the ground. Fear has been the gospel of my life. It has stopped me from taking risks, trying something new, being adventurous, and being myself. But, where did this fear originate? If all I can remember is fear, then it must have begun before I have any memories of it. It would be nice if I could put my finger on an exact moment or a certain event and say, "Ah......that's it," but learning about myself doesn't work that way. It's never that easy, but I am learning that it's worth it.

Flashbacks

I've gone back in my memories and focused on the times that I was afraid. I can remember when I went to the dentist for the first time. From my viewpoint this was a big man that towered over my tiny four-year-old body. I don't remember what he said to me, but he helped me up into the big chair, counted my teeth and gave me a toothbrush. I climbed down from the chair and went into the next room where my mom was, and I fainted. When I woke up, I remember still clinging to the toothbrush in my hand. I left with a very deep fear of all dentists. This fear has been with me now for forty years. I've always blamed that first dentist for frightening me so deeply, although I couldn't remember anything that had specifically scared me. Recently, I have found the reason for this fear through the several flashbacks I've had. I have remembered someone holding my mouth open with his fingers so I wouldn't bite him. This had to have happened to me before I went to the dentist that first time. I know now that it was his fingers that caused me to be so afraid, but it wasn't his fault. My memory revealed that someone in my family had orally sexually abused me. So if any man touches my mouth in that way, I panic. I have bitten dentists and passed out. Needless to say, I have only gone to the dentist when necessary.

There was another time when I was a child that I passed out. I was six and I had a loose tooth. It was really bothering me, so I told my mom about it. She was in the middle of cooking dinner and said that I should have dad check it for me. I can still remember the fear inside as I walked up to my dad's chair, where he was reading the paper. First of all, I knew that he didn't like to be bothered and second of all, I was afraid that it would hurt if he pulled it. I told him about the tooth, he reached up and touched it quickly with his finger and said that it wasn't ready to come out. I turned to walk away and the next thing I remember was waking up on the floor in front of his chair. As I came to, I heard him yelling at me for being so clumsy and he called me an ox. It seems that I had hit the footrest of the recliner as I went down and it had disturbed his reading. Even when he realized that I had fainted, he didn't try to comfort me or apologize. I felt so stupid for being so afraid. I never let my dad touch my teeth again.

As the flashbacks have brought the reason for my fears to the surface, I have been trying to be compassionate to the little girl inside of me that has been living in fear for so long. Now I know it was not stupid to be afraid; I was protecting myself the only way I knew how. Knowing that someone used me in that way, especially when I was just a small child, sickens me. I have grieved the loss of my innocence. I shake and cry at the vulgarity of it. It should not have happened, yet it did, but, because I know the truth it has helped me to put the fear into perspective. The memories I had repressed are helping me to put the pieces together. There are many things I've been afraid of that are a result of what happened so long ago. I am not crazy and I have the right to be scared, along with the right to be angry. This fear does not have to control my life any longer. I am learning how to control it.

The most intense fear that I have known occurs during a flashback. I never know when my mind will be triggered, but I have learned to recognize the signs of one beginning. This gives me time to alert someone from my support system so I am not alone.

As many flashbacks as I've experienced, God has blessed me by always having someone nearby that knows how to help me. I have never had a flashback when I've been by myself. Trusting God with this is comforting to me and also to my husband, Duane, since he worries that he might not be there when I need him. When the memories surface, I definitely need someone, because I am a small child once again and very afraid.

A familiar story, a particular phrase, an inappropriate touch, the smell of smoke or someone that resembles the person that hurt me have triggered my flashbacks. The first sign that a memory is trying to come to the surface is that my right hand begins to shake. As hard as I try to control it, the shaking continues. I feel sick to my stomach. Suddenly my head begins to hurt and pound with extreme pain and the shaking in my hand spreads to my whole body. Within moments I begin to cry uncontrollably and I always need to sit on the floor with my legs crossed. The fear that I'm feeling keeps me from speaking about what's happening to me. I rock and cry while my support person holds me. They constantly remind me that I'm safe and that no one can hurt me anymore. As I've become more familiar with the pattern of a flashback, I am able to say what is needed as the memory is returning. In my little girl voice, I tell the things that are happening to me at that moment. Eventually, the memory begins to fade and the shaking subsides. When I feel once again that I'm an adult the memory becomes complete and very real. Then I cry, from the pain of this happening to me and for the little girl who went through so much alone. When I think of how afraid she must have been, I want to hold her close and tell her how proud I am of her for being so strong. After a while, the fear and sorrow are replaced by a deep sense of peace. Each flashback brings me one step closer to knowing what the secrets are that have been kept from me. Once the secrets are revealed, there will be no more fear and my little girl will be forever safe within me.

Afraid of Being Angry

Fear creeps up on me silently, sneaking up on me when I'm not expecting it. It can be disguised and hidden in an opportunity for me to help someone else. This happens often in my work as a chaplain at the hospital. One situation in particular I will always remember because the intensity of the fear stayed with me long after it ended. It began at the start of my shift early one Saturday morning. When I arrived, the night chaplain called me from the emergency room. He explained that paramedics had brought in a three-month-old baby that was pronounced dead just moments before. These were words that I dreaded hearing. Every death is hard for me, but when it's a baby I want to just scream and beg God to help me understand. I prayed as I walked down the long hall to ER. I asked God to give me strength to be with this family in their time of need, help me to stay present to them and to give them His comfort.

As I went into the trauma room, I saw the chaplain sitting with the mother of the baby. She was clasping her son to her and screaming. In that moment, I wanted to run away rather than to face this horrible grief. In the next moment, my heart was filled with her anguish and I went to be at her side. My heart continued to break as I realized that this mom was very young. I found out later that she was only seventeen years old. As more family members arrived, it became obvious that this was a very dysfunctional family. No one seemed to have enough strength to help each other. They were each lost in their own grief. I learned that there were several family members that lived together in the same house and they each shared in the care of the baby. While the baby was in their care it was very common for him to sleep in bed with them instead of in his crib. This included the mother, but she insisted that the baby had been in his crib when she found him not breathing.

As the truth was later revealed that the baby had indeed been in the bed with his mother, my fears for the cause of the baby's death were confirmed. He had been smothered. This was a horrible, tragic accident and it should not have happened. None of the adults in the house had been responsible enough to realize how dangerous this could be. It was about this time that my responsibility burdens began to kick in. I really had to struggle to not take over the situation and take care of everyone. I concentrated on the mother and helped her to hold her baby, to rock him, to cry over him and to scream away some of the pain. Throughout several hours of intense grief, I kept pushing away the thoughts I was having in the back of my mind, so I could be present with the family. I knew that I would have time to process my issues later.

After the family had left the hospital, I saw the baby one last time. As I pulled the curtain in the doorway, anger overcame me. Then came fear. The thoughts that I had pushed away came rushing back at me. I was angry at the lack of responsibility for this child. A beautiful little boy had died because of ignorance. I tried to understand why God had taken this child. Did He take him to save him from growing up with this family? Did the baby die in order for the mother to learn from her mistake? If God would save this baby from a childhood of hurt and betrayal, then why wasn't I saved from mine? For days I tried to process these questions. I wondered where the anger and fear were coming from. I tried the usual ways that help me to work through an intense situation like this one, such as talking with my peers, journaling, sitting quietly with God. I became frustrated that I couldn't resolve it. I felt that something was blocking me from knowing this fear, and that God wanted me to face it and learn from it. He also wanted me to receive the answers to my questions.

On the following Wednesday morning, when our teacher Urias arrived for class, he asked me how I was. When I looked at him with tears in my eyes and said, "Lousy," he arranged for us to talk right after class. I was grateful because I knew I needed him to help me face whatever was there. We went to his office and I began telling him more about the baby's death. I was talking very rapidly about everything that had happened and I began to cry as I told him about the questions in my heart. Suddenly, I realized that I had known that some day I would face this moment—the moment when I would come face to face with my anger and ask God why. I was terrified of what would happen to me if I admitted that I was angry with Him.

One of the things I love about Urias is his strong, deep, comforting voice. The tone is husky, low and feels like velvet to me. The first thing he asked me to do was to try to relax. When I'm upset, my breathing becomes very rapid, which in turn makes me feel more upset. Urias helped me to concentrate on taking deep breaths as he counted to four with each inhale, hold and exhale. As my breathing became easier, I began to relax and closed my eyes. In order for me to focus on what was causing the fear I was feeling, Urias helped me to think back to earlier times in my life. He asked me questions about what I remembered at these times and who was with me. When he asked me what life was like when I was eleven or twelve, I talked of the responsibility of taking care of my brothers and sister, doing housework, laundry, making dinners and taking care of my mom after every argument with my dad.

Then we talked about my life as a four-year-old. I had a distinct memory of sitting on the floor with my coloring book. My dad was in the other room taking care of my baby brother. I felt afraid as my dad's anger became out of control. He was trying to change my brother's messy diaper, and he was mad. This memory seemed to fit with one of the flashbacks I've had where I feel myself hiding under my brother's crib. I'm sobbing and crying, but trying to be quiet as I hide. My brother is screaming and I see my dad's shoes as he's standing in front of the crib. My fear is very intense and it grows as my dad's anger grows.

Anger and fear seem to be one and the same for me. I'm afraid of anyone's anger, including my own, and I'm angry when I feel afraid. Urias and I talked about this as he tried to help me answer my own questions. First of all, he told me that God does not take babies. He welcomes them when tragic things in life happen, but He does not take them. Secondly, God did not "leave" me in my situation. He was with me every moment, I just hadn't realized that yet. Then Urias asked me the big question, "Why do you feel afraid of God knowing your anger?" "I'm the responsible one," was my answer. I've always been the responsible one. When the younger kids didn't behave, as they should, I was the first one to get hit with the belt. I was told since I was the oldest and was responsible for the other kids and couldn't keep them in line, then I was to blame. Hearing that made me angry, but I was afraid to express that anger for fear of getting hit harder with the belt. Anger and fear had caused me physical and emotional pain. Anger and fear had attempted to murder my soul. It was then that I realized what I needed to learn from the baby's death. I was afraid of expressing my anger toward God for fear of what my punishment would be. God wanted me to understand that I didn't need to be afraid of Him. Urias asked me if I was angry with the baby's mother. When I told him no, he wanted to know why. I explained to him that she is only a child herself. If I saw her again I would want to put my arms around her and comfort her, instead of judging her. In my heart I knew that God was teaching me that He is doing the same for me. I needed an experience like this one in order to really feel how powerful His love is for me. It surpasses all fear and anger, and it gives me permission to be myself and to express my feelings openly.

As my time with Urias came to an end, I was much calmer and at peace. My questions had been answered for the moment, but I know more questions will come. With each question and the answer that follows, I am learning more about myself and the person that I'm becoming. Fear does not have to rule my life any longer. I'm moving beyond it. There is no fear when I am in the Glory of God's love.

Free to be myself

For most of my life, fear has had an unrelenting power over me. It has taken away my freedom to explore the possibilities that life had to offer me. That night when I heard my dad tell me that I was clumsy and an ox was not the first or the only time. When I was very young, I remember dad calling me his pumpkin. Sometime before I turned six, everything changed. I was no longer his little girl. I was the one that was always bumping into things or falling down. There was no way for me to understand the hurt I felt because of his words. I felt that I was always disappointing him. My father was the most important person in my life and I would do anything to please him. There were so many things that I tried just so he would notice me. I took baton lessons, tried out for cheerleading, sang in the choir, played basketball and much more. Not only did he never attend any of my events, but his words kept me from enjoying myself fully.

It was the fear of anyone calling me clumsy that kept me from giving my all. Several people told me to just loosen up and have fun, but I couldn't, I had to be perfect. My body moved like a robot, making every move precision-like; otherwise I would look clumsy. My arms and legs were stiff. I couldn't even smile, because I was concentrating so hard on being perfect. The words from someone I loved had caused fear to paralyze me. The comments from him when I didn't receive high marks or a trophy caused fear to paralyze my soul.

Now that I know why fear has always ruled my life, it's easier to understand and let it go. I've found that when you turn the letters around in the word *fear*, it becomes very close to the word *free*. That's what I feel now, free. Free to take risks, to try something new, to have adventures and to be who I'm supposed to be. The most wonderful part of going through my fears is that my little girl is also becoming free. Together we are celebrating our freedom. Fear will never again stop me from realizing my potential. God has performed a miracle and set my soul free. I no longer have to be perfect for my Father to notice me, because I am already perfect in His eyes.

Reflecting on Our Fears

When we think about what fear has done to us, we get angry. Fear gripped us in its tight vices and held us captive in its claws, squeezing the life out of us. It robbed us of the pleasures of life and killed our joy. Fear brought death, rather than the new life for which we longed. When we consider our fears, we are drawn to the story of the disciples and Jesus crossing the Sea of Galilee when a terrible storm arose. Jesus was in the boat with them, but He was sleeping. They feared for their lives when the boat began to sink. They woke Jesus, begging Him to save them. "What little faith you have," He said. He then spoke to the storm. The waves ceased and became calm (Matthew 8:23-27).

Many things in our lives take our focus away from Jesus. One day, Jesus came to the disciples, walking on the water. He invited Peter to come to Him. Peter stepped out of the boat, but was afraid. His faith in Jesus wavered, he looked down at the water and began to sink. Jesus has invited us to walk with Him in faith, taking the risk to step out of the boat. Our faith in Him keeps us afloat as long as our eyes are on Him. When we look away we are overcome by our fears. Yet, when we call to Him, He saves us (Matthew 14:22-33).

Throughout our life experiences Jesus is with us. We may think that He is sleeping, but He is always aware of what is happening to us. If the storm had not been fierce, the disciples would not have experienced Jesus calming the waves. We believe that God does not cause our struggles, but when we are faced with a crisis, God is able to guide us through our fears and we become stronger as we go through the experience by keeping our eyes focused only upon Him.

Many times, God provides someone in our lives to walk alongside us through our fears and struggles. Esther was a young girl, living with her uncle Mordecai, when word came that the king was searching for a wife. It was ordered that all the girls of marrying age in the land would be brought before the king. This included Esther. Fear overcame her as she was forced to leave the safety of her uncle's home. Mordecai was also afraid, but for a different reason. Everywhere, Jews were being persecuted for their faith. The king did not know that

Esther was a Jew. Mordecai encouraged Esther to keep this truth a secret because he feared for her life.

The king was very taken by Esther's beauty and took her for his wife. She lived within the walls of the kingdom and was not allowed to visit Mordecai. God knew that Esther needed her uncle's support and love. Every day, Mordecai came to the walls and waited, hoping that Esther would see him and know that he was near.

On one of his visits to the kingdom, Mordecai was able to speak to Esther. He told her that a friend of the king, Haman, was planning to convince the king to destroy all of the Jews. Knowing how much the king respected Esther, Mordecai prayed that she could change his mind. Her life would be in danger, but the lives of the entire Jewish community depended on Esther's courage.

Esther was terrified of confronting the king, but Mordecai encouraged and offered his support. He could not be at her side, but he could pray and stay nearby. Before asking the king for time together, Esther asked Mordecai to spread the word to the community, pleading for them to fast and pray for her to have courage. For several days, all of the Jews prayed that God would help Esther to convince the king to save their lives. The time came for the meeting. Esther revealed her secret and begged her husband to look kindly on her community. The king was overwhelmed at her courage and granted her request out of respect for her. Haman was killed and the Jewish people were saved (the book of Esther).

There are times in our lives when we must face the monster in the closet. We can't run away. God gives us wonderful examples of courage and strength in the Bible to help us overcome our fears in spite of the dangers. His presence can be found in caring people in our lives that will stand by and encourage us. Fear does not need to paralyze us; instead it can become our incentive and the fuel for our determination to confront the monster. With God's help, we can defeat it!

Fuel for your journey

1. Which story caused you to think of your own experiences? Why?

2. How does it make you feel?

3. What would you like to say to God right now?

4. Who can you share these feelings with?

CHAPTER THREE

Shame

Unworthy of Love

Guilt and shame seem to be one and the same, but we have learned that guilt is recognizing our actions as failures. Shame is believing that we are the failure. If guilt is about asking for forgiveness, then shame is about asking for wholeness. In order to become whole, we first need to acknowledge the feelings that shame creates. Shame causes us to feel unworthy, like a worm crawling around on its belly. Shame is being overlooked. It's being taken for granted. We are the dirty laundry that is thrown into the corner. Shame is a feeling we harbor deep within the alcoves of our souls. We are unaware of its controlling power. It is the unseen presence that causes us to feel worthless, unloved, unappreciated, unrecognized. Shame slithers through and invades the very being of our soul, causing us to feel like a nobody, a person of no value. It blocks out

God's light and destroys our life. It withers and distorts our personalities and causes us to feel rotten. We are left pale and lifeless.

Lori

Shopping Day

When I was growing up, shame became closely associated with guilt. "You should be ashamed of yourself," was a statement that I heard over and over again. When I hit my brother, when I had a C on my report card, when my chores were not done, when I wore makeup, when my dad was angry, when my mom had a headache and especially if I told anyone about something that happened at home. Shame was pounded into me. Everything seemed to be my fault. I admit that I was guilty of some of these things, but as I look back, the things I did were normal for my age, since I was just a child. However, causing my mom to have a headache was not my fault. At the end of every summer, we would all pile into the car with mom to go school clothes shopping. There was a very limited time to shop and buy clothes, shoes and school supplies for four children in one day. The shopping day was usually only a couple of days before school started, due to my mom's procrastination. It would be late morning by the time we actually left home for the stores. After waiting all morning to leave, we were already on each other's nerves and the fighting had begun. We would usually go to a store that carried a variety of clothing for the whole family, with the plan of going from one department to the next. The first stops were the easiest to do, since my sister was the youngest, then the boys wore about the same sizes, but by the time it was my turn the turmoil had really begun. By now, we were all hungry, hot and tired. The boys were bored and my sister was whining. No one had the patience that I had while the others had shopped. I had put up with their grumbling and kept them in line and now when my time came they were at their worst. Mom's patience was already wearing very thin and she kept telling me to hurry. I was at the age where what I wore was extremely important to my self-esteem, so I would fit in at school. Having to hurriedly pick out my school clothes became torment, since everything I liked, Mom didn't like. Finally, she would just pick the things out for me so we could leave. I was so unhappy with what was bought and I sulked all the way home. I remember promising myself that one day I would go shopping on my own, but that day seemed very far away. When we arrived home, Mom told us to take our new things to our rooms and stay there. We were told that we had given her a horrible headache and she needed to lie down. And, so would end our day of shopping.

It could have been so different. It was not our fault that we needed new clothes for school. We had all grown over the summers so the clothes were a necessity. Money was tight and Mom had a very limited budget with which to work with. Everything we bought had to be on sale or on clearance. I still shop that way today for my family, but occasionally I've purchased something really special at the regular price because it was what the kids wanted. It's extremely hard for me to do that for myself, however. The shame I feel when I consider buying something that's not on sale, even though I may really like it, is unbearable. I feel that I don't deserve it. Remembering the shopping trips when I was a child helps me to understand why I treat myself this way and to overcome the shame that doesn't belong to me. But when I was told over and over again that it was such a burden to buy me what I needed and that I caused sickness, anger and headaches, the shame attached itself to my soul.

Growing Up a Failure

The physical punishment that I received as a child has resulted in a very deep sense of shame within me. Being hit with a belt, being told that I was bad, being forced to apologize for things I had not done have left permanent wounds on my heart and has touched every part of my life in some way. When I was little, I learned to be aware of the tension between my parents. As the oldest, I tried to make things better out of fear of being punished. I became the housekeeper that picked up after everyone, did the laundry, made meals. I took on the role of mother to my younger siblings, especially with my little sister. When Mom and Dad fought, I was the one who comforted my mom. As frightened as I was of the fights they had, I would go to my mom and sit with her, telling her that it would be okay. It should have been the other way around. She should have been comforting me. But, as hard as I tried to keep peace, I failed many, many times. By the age of twelve, I thought of myself as a failure.

I can still remember the sounds, the stings and the humiliation of being hit with the belt. I had become nothing more than a possession to my parents, something they could use to release their anger and frustrations. It seemed that there was nothing I could do to prevent the beatings from happening, but I always knew when it was coming. The tension usually started building early in the day. We were typical children doing typical things, but everything seemed to irritate my mom. She used a great deal of yelling and spanking to try to control us. By suppertime, she had made a mental list of each time we had made her angry.

Dinner became a time of fear for us several nights each week. Dad was late coming home very often and the later he was, the greater the chance of us being punished. The food would be ready, but Mom didn't let us eat until Dad came home. Some nights we waited for hours to eat because he was late. I can still remember her standing at the kitchen window, watching the road for his car, with her arms crossed and getting angrier as the minutes went by. Sometimes there was a good reason for him to be late because he was working, but other times he didn't come home right away, he went to the bar instead. So we waited, knowing what was to come.

When, at last, Mom saw his car coming down the road, she hurriedly threw supper on the table and we quickly sat down. We were so hungry by this time, but we still had to wait until Dad sat down to the table to eat. Supper always began with prayers, which we said very quickly. Mom served Dad first and then us. When she finally sat down, she was very angry and the litany of things we had done wrong all day came pouring out. It was very hard for me to eat while this was going on. Eventually I developed a stomach problem, which still bothers me today when I'm overly stressed. Instead of facing her anger with him, my mom found it easier to make him just as angry as she was. She was out for revenge. By the middle of the meal, she had achieved her goal. He was very angry, yelling at us and pounding his fists on the table. If one of us started to cry, it pushed him over the edge and he stood up and took off his belt. One by one, we were told to go to him. I was always first because I was the oldest. I was so afraid, it seemed my feet wouldn't move. I didn't understand what I had done that would cause me to be punished with the belt. We were all crying by this time and the longer we hesitated going to him the madder he became. I finally made my way over to him, crying and shaking uncontrollably, instinctively placing my hands behind me. He grabbed me by the front of my neck to hold me still and told me to move my hands. I did, only because I knew that I would get hit more if I didn't. I don't remember how many times he hit me each time, but the older we were the more we received. As he hit me he told me that I was the oldest, the responsible one and I was getting this punishment because I didn't make the others behave. I believed him and I was ashamed.

My brothers came next and then my sister. She was very little and fortunately by the time Dad had gone through the rest of us, his anger had lessened, but she was still very scared. While the boys were getting their punishment, my sister clung to me and cried. I would have done anything to spare her, but I couldn't, I was helpless. The only one that could stop it would have been my mom and she didn't. She stood there watching as each of her children were being punished. As an adult, I'm trying to understand the reason for her actions, but at the time, all I wanted was for my mother to make it stop. I wondered what was going through her mind. How could she do this? Did she justify it because she had received the same kind of punishments when she was a child? Was she afraid that Dad would take out his anger on her? Were we really that bad? I survived by convincing myself that this was normal and that all kids were treated this way by their parents.

When the punishments were over and Dad had put his belt back on, we were told to finish our supper. We were upset and crying, but we had to sit at the table until we ate everything on our plates. Mom said that Dad worked very hard to put food in our mouths and we weren't going to waste it. My parents then finished their meals calmly in silence. It was so hard for us to eat, but we forced it down. When we were done and had cleaned off the table, Mom told us to go and apologize to our dad for making him angry. It was our fault that he hit us with the belt and we had to say we were sorry to him. Again, one by one, we lined up with me being the first. We walked into the living room where he was sitting in his chair reading the paper. Once again, I felt that my feet wouldn't move, I was so afraid of making him mad once more. Mom kept urging us on. We each stood before him and said, "I'm sorry, Dad, for making you hit me." He never acknowledged us. He didn't put the paper down, but continued reading. In those moments, I felt I was drowning in shame. I was so bad that he couldn't even look at me. His actions made me feel worthless and that I didn't exist. Each time this happened I felt that I lost more of his love for me, so I tried even harder to get that love back. I have never succeeded. I feel the shame of failure once again.

It has taken me a very long time to come to some sort of understanding of why my parents did the things they did. Even though I had convinced myself when I was little that the punishments were normal, I believe that deep down I knew the truth. I was ashamed of being in a family like ours. It would have been more horrible than the punishment was if anyone had found out. So I kept the secrets. I never even told my closest friends. It has only been in the last few years that I have talked about the darker times of my childhood. Everything that I have learned has helped me to know myself better and has answered many of my questions about my childhood. While nothing can justify the abuse for any child, understanding the history of the abusers can bring closure, peace and eventually forgiveness.

I have always known that my parents' childhoods were traumatic for them. They have never discussed the details, but I believe that I was treated as they were treated. The "family traditions" that began many generations ago and handed down over the years, were all my parents knew. This was the way to raise children. But, even though they felt they were doing the right thing, they held a great deal of shame because of it. We were told to never talk to anyone about what happened at home. The opinions of others were extremely important, so whenever we were out in public, we were expected to behave like the perfect little family that sat in the front pew of church every week so others would not know what was actually going on in our home.

This threat of exposing the family secrets may have been the reason why punishments with the belt finally came to an end. I was fifteen years old when my father hit us for the last time. It was summertime and we were in the front yard playing.

My parents came out of the house and Dad used his belt on us as cars drove by. We were all humiliated once again. But, it was the last time for that kind of abuse on any of us. The reason that it never happened again has never been discussed. I believe that when they realized that someone had seen what happened, the shame was enough to make it stop. Even though it has been almost thirty years since the last time I felt a belt against my skin, the trauma and the emotional scars are still very fresh in my memory. Wounds like this can take a lifetime to heal.

What About Me?

One of the horrible things about shame is that once it has invaded your soul it becomes a foundation to build upon. Living with the heaviness of it eventually seems normal. My first memory of feeling shameful was when I was about four years old. I had one of those big plastic balls that kids like to play with. Somehow, I found that sitting on the ball and moving back and forth felt really good. Yet, even as young as I was, I knew that it was wrong to do this. I would hide behind the couch or a chair each time. This behavior is very common in children that have been sexually abused. It's a way of relieving the stress and tension from the trauma inflicted upon them. What I was doing was masturbating. I have been so ashamed of this that I had never told anyone about it. Finally, I was able to say it out loud to my therapist about a year ago. Once again, when I was little I thought this was normal behavior. Now I know that it was a symptom of the horrible things that were happening to me. Amazingly, no one seemed to notice or if they did, they chose to ignore it. As a result, the abuse continued. This was my foundation of shame.

Physical, sexual and emotional abuse caused me to heap shame upon shame, layer after layer until it took over my identity. I became a person that was comfortable being a failure. It seemed like everything I did or every decision I made was wrong. I couldn't be the obedient daughter, the dependable older sister, the good student any longer. I had given up. I just lived day after day waiting for someone to rescue me. I wanted someone to see the real me, and love me for who I was. During my last year of high school, I wished every night as I cried myself to sleep that there was somebody somewhere that would love me. It seemed hopeless to me since the shame had wiped out my self-esteem and caused me to be very shy.

Graduation was coming and I was very relieved to be almost done with school. At this point I had no clue as to what I wanted to do with my life. I had given some thought to a nursing career because I felt taking care of people was something that I was good at. It was hard for me to decide and then my dad had an accident and the decision was made for me. There was a fire at the garage where he was working. Fortunately the fire was quickly put out, but he suffered third degree burns over most of his body. He was rushed to the hospital, where he spent the next six weeks in the burn unit. Since my dad was self-employed, the family income came to a halt. I decided to put off going to school and went to work instead. As soon as I graduated I was working full time and had forgotten about a nursing career.

During the summer after graduation I was working and still keeping up with my responsibilities at home. My dad had recovered from the accident and things had returned to the way they had always been. One of my friends that had moved into an apartment a few months before called one day and invited me over. She told me that her roommate had to move out unexpectedly, so she was looking for someone to share the apartment with until her lease ended in the fall. And she asked me. I was so excited and said yes right away. We had been friends since kindergarten, the apartment was affordable and only a mile from home. I was sure my parents would approve of my living on my own for a few months. I went home and started to pack.

Later that evening Mom arrived home and I found her in the kitchen to tell her the news. As I was explaining the details, my excitement was replaced with fear. She became very angry and said that I didn't have the right to tell my friend that I would move in. She would not allow me to leave home, end of discussion. Then she turned away from me and continued making dinner. I stood there watching her. I couldn't believe that she would do this to me. This was so important to me and she wouldn't even listen to me or try to understand. She had always controlled everything in my life, but this was different. I was eighteen now. Didn't I have any say about my future? As I thought that I would never be able to get away, I began to panic. I left the kitchen without saying another word and went to my room.

For the first time in my life I wanted to rebel. I wanted to get away and be free. This opportunity was too good for me to miss. I had to go. Somewhere from within me I felt an enormous amount of courage and urgency. Quickly I threw all of my clothes into garbage bags and stuffed my purse with as much as I could. I was leaving and no one was going to stop me. I grabbed the bags, walked down the hall, through the living room and out the front door. Before I got to my car, I could hear her screaming.

I will never forget the sound of her voice, yelling at me to stop. She came running out of the house crying hysterically. My little sister, who was about twelve, had no idea what was happening and came running outside also. I hurriedly threw the bags in the car, got in and locked my doors. The fear of what Mom would do to me to make me stop overcame me. My hands were shaking so hard that I couldn't get the key in the ignition to start the car. By this time she was pounding on the window and screaming that I had better not leave, that she would never forgive me. She was hitting the glass so hard that I thought she would break it. I wanted so badly to start that car and drive away. I tried putting the keys in again and this time I did it. As I turned the key, I looked up and there was my sister, standing in front of the car, pleading with me not to go. She was crying so hard. She needed me and I needed her. In that moment I knew that I had lost. I couldn't leave. I turned the engine off, laid my head on the steering wheel and cried.

I don't remember how long I sat there before unlocking the doors and letting my mom in. Everything seemed to be moving in slow motion. Once again, I was defeated. My mom had succeeded in making me a nobody, a person of no worth, someone that was not allowed to make any decisions on her own. She pulled me out of the car and she may have hit me, I don't remember. It didn't matter anyway, the damage had already been done. When we went into the house, she made me call my friend and tell her that I couldn't move in. Shame was oozing from every part of me as I dialed her number. I knew that I had let her down and I was more worried about her than I was myself. Fortunately, she said she understood, but we never talked about it again.

My mom then went back to finishing supper as if nothing had happened. I went to my room, sat down on the floor and sobbed. My sister came in but I told her to go away. When Dad arrived home, I was told that supper was on the table. As soon as I sat down, Mom began telling Dad what I had done. He started telling me how bad I was to have made Mom angry. After that statement I was even more devastated and wanted to scream, "But, what about me?" but I sat in silence. I know that he gave me some kind of punishment, but I don't remember what it was. Nothing mattered to me anymore. I was weak and had lost the little bit of courage I had received earlier. It had been ripped from me and left a gaping, oozing wound of shame in its place.

Baggage

At this time in my life, I didn't have much faith in God. From my point of view, He certainly wasn't involved in my life. I didn't even believe that He knew who I was. Looking back on it now, I can definitely see His Presence in every moment. It was my self-esteem and feelings of unworthiness that were blocking my vision of Him. I used to dream and plan my future, but never had the courage to do anything about it. That all changed when Duane entered my life. He is the reason that I know God was watching over me. After having gone through the physical and emotional abuse of my childhood, I became very desperate to get away, but I knew I couldn't do it alone. A few months after I had tried to leave home, Duane and I met on a blind date and have been together ever since. He was the person that I had been wishing for every night when I cried myself to sleep. God must have known that as vulnerable as I was, I would have gone with any man that came along. So He didn't send just any man, He sent my soul mate. Now, I realize that the wishes I had been asking for were in fact prayers, and God had heard me.

Within months Duane and I were married and I was positive that all my problems were behind me. What I discovered, however, was that I had not outrun my past because I had not dealt with my hurt and pain. When I left my parents' house, I unknowingly packed my shame with all of my belongings. Some of the painful issues from my childhood remained packed away for many years. Eventually, as I became stronger and more confident in who I was, the feelings began to surface, one by one. This strength that I needed had actually been inside of me the whole time, but it was hidden and covered with a heavy blanket of shame. When I came to the point of surrender to God, He began helping me by moving away the shame so I could see the light of my strength underneath. In the beginning, it felt like I was standing at the base of a long, dark and scary tunnel. It was the light of my strength shining at the end, even though I could barely see it, that kept me moving forward and not turning back.

Long before I was able to see that light or believe that I could ask God for His help, the feelings I had buried so long ago surfaced many times. They came disguised as low self-esteem, shyness and unworthiness. I became very dependent on Duane. I couldn't make any decisions on my own, even small ones such as what to have for dinner. The only thing that I really wanted was kids. Taking care of others had become my identity. It was the only one I was comfortable with. I believed that the only way I would be truly happy was to be a mom. Being Duane's wife and Jason and Krystina's mom has made me incredibly happy. I can't imagine who I would be without them. But, that happiness could not heal the damage that had been done so long before. It was still with me. It overshadowed everything and it was robbing me of the joy in my life.

This damage manifested itself through the many jobs I had. Since I didn't have a formal education, I was limited in the kind of work that I would enjoy doing. I settled for jobs that I didn't like because I believed that I wouldn't qualify for anything better. After a while a pattern developed with each new position. First, in the interview I would answer their questions in what I had guessed they wanted to hear. I was always afraid and nervous of starting a new job, but determined that this time they would see the skills I had to offer and would appreciate me. I learned the job quickly and always offered to do more. This would lead to the second phase of the pattern, in which I began to feel used and taken for granted. My low self-esteem required constant positive feedback in order for me to feel comfortable and needed in my position. When this didn't happen, I became hurt and angry. Eventually, the pattern would end in frustration and I would quit and move on to another job. But, the results were always the same, the pattern continued.

Even though I was in this vicious employment cycle, I didn't have the confidence to apply for better positions. Every time I attempted, the qualifications for jobs that I knew I would like made me feel even more worthless. They required college degrees. At some of the places that hired me, I worked alongside of others doing the same exact job, doing as well as they did and in some cases even better, but I was making less money. They had degrees and I did not. This made me extremely angry and dissatisfied with the employer, so I would eventually quit. In one instance, my supervisor told me that they would increase my pay rate by 25 cents an hour if I could prove to them that I was enrolled in a college to earn my degree. I had just received perfect marks on my evaluation from her and yet she held the degree in front of me like a farmer holds a carrot in front of a donkey to get it to move.

The shame that I have carried because I raised a family instead of pursuing a degree has caused me a great deal of pain. I feel angry when I know that I'm not considered because I don't have a piece of paper on the wall, even though I am fully capable of doing the work. I also feel that getting a degree should be a personal decision and not one that is coerced by someone else. This shame has kept me from sharing the gifts that God has given me with others. It has made me feel that I am only a mom or only a hostess or only a cashier or only a high school graduate. I should have felt pride in having accomplished these things in my life. But, the impact of the words, "No, you don't qualify," on my soul are like a sledge-hammer driving the nails in a little deeper each time. Pounding my self-esteem into non-existence. Drowning my confidence in the murky waters of shame.

As I moved in and out of these jobs, I found myself wanting more. When God revealed to me that His plan for me was to be in chaplaincy and help others in their time of need, I began to feel a strength that would help me to overcome the shame of not having an education. I called the hospital to inquire about the C.P.E. Program. The educator asked me if I had a degree, since it's required for admission. The new strength I had found raised up inside of me and I heard myself telling him that I didn't have a degree, but I wasn't going to let that stop me this time. I asked if there was any other way. His next question for me was, "Are you Catholic?" When I said that I was, he suggested that I call the Diocese for information on the Lay Ministry Program. My self-esteem soared when I received the call from Sister Jo inviting me to join the class. I had been accepted! The education that I've earned at the Diocese and C.P.E. have given me the confidence I need to continue my education.

My Support System

As much as I had grown in strength and self-confidence from the Diocese program and C.P.E., the pain and hurt came crashing in on me once again when I began having flashbacks. About five months into my education through C.P.E., the first memory returned during a group session with my peers. I was extremely frightened because I didn't know what was happening to me. Thankfully, God had placed me with people that recognized the pain I was having and more importantly, I felt safe enough to allow the pain to surface. They each stayed with me, assuring me that what I was reliving was in the past and they believed me. As I finally began to calm down, my friends circled around me and prayed for me to have peace. In a matter of a few moments, all the strength I had gained seemed to disappear. My blanket of shame had covered the light once again.

The dirty feeling of shame has tried again and again to make me believe that I am less than a person. During a flashback that happened with Sara at my side, the memory was coming back in bits and pieces. I was crying and afraid. Then, suddenly in my mind, I saw a "snapshot" of my dad's shoes. Instantly I knew what God was trying to tell me. I was afraid of my dad. As Sara held me, I told her what I had realized. She rocked me and let me cry. When I felt better, I went to the ladies room to wash my face. I was horrified at what I saw in the mirror. It was my dad's face. There was such a deep, dark feeling of shame that I couldn't even look at myself. I have a very strong resemblance to my dad and have always been unhappy with how I look. Now, in my mind I saw the person I was afraid of instead of me.

When I left the restroom, Sr. Anne was in our office. Anne is on staff at the hospital as a chaplain and she is a very good friend. I went to her and she gathered me into her arms. As she hugged me, I told her what I had remembered and that I couldn't see myself in the mirror. By this time, I was sobbing and hiccupping like a child. Anne took me by the shoulders and made me look at her. She then tenderly held my face and told me, "You are you. You are not your father. You couldn't be like him, if you tried. God loves you and I love you for who you are and you are beautiful." Anne's words lifted that blanket of shame from me. She gave me hope that I would someday see myself as she sees me.

This feeling of shame is very common for victims of sexual abuse. We feel that it was somehow our fault, that we could have stopped it and that the people that love us will turn away when they hear the truth of what happened. All of these things are not true, but it's hard to make any abuse survivor believe it. My recovery is an ongoing process, in which support from others is vital. I know that there is always someone who is willing to face the pain with me. If there is anyone out there that is going through this alone, I encourage you to reach out and find somebody. You are not alone. There are millions of others who are facing the same tragedy. And there is someone waiting to love you through it.

I will never forget those words from Anne that day, nor will I forget the countless times that my support people have been there for me. Their love and devotion have been blessings to me from God. The fear that I had of losing their love has not materialized. In fact, I feel the love more deeply, since we have connected in such a personal way. In the twenty-five years that we have been married, Duane and I have gone through many difficult things, but nothing compares to this. Recently, I received a dozen roses from him because I was having a hard day. The card read, "Together we are strong." We have gained this strength by following God, taking one day at a time and loving each other. We will continue to move forward with everything we've learned. I do not own any of this shame. Those who do will have to own it themselves. I will not carry it for them any longer. I am free.

Sara

The Invisible Giant

Shame makes me feel unworthy like a worm slithering along on my belly. I also think of shame as being an invisible giant in my life. The giant occupies an enormous amount of space in my soul. It affects how I feel about myself and how I interact with others. It was invisible because I was not aware of its presence. It has been through the C.P.E. experience that I realized the power shame had over me. Although I was well acquainted with the feelings shame produced, I did not have a real handle on the impact it had in my life. When I began the program, we were told that our patients and their families would become our best teachers. I began to understand the full implication of that comment when I dealt with an elderly woman who struggled with depression. I made numerous attempts to rescue her from her pit of despair. I felt as though every time I would almost get her out of the hole she would fall back down. I could not handle her depression because I also struggled with depression and it was shameful to admit that to others. I could not face my own depression because it made me feel unworthy of God's love or anyone else's love. As a result I could not be present with the patient.

My earliest feeling of shame was experienced in Sunday School when I was about four years old. We were standing in a straight line and had completed singing the offering song. My teachers had asked me a question and I was too shy to reply. I stood in silence, my heart pounding in my chest. The teachers leaned down and looked into my face, but the only reply they received was silence. Frustrated with my noncompliance, one of them said, "Did the cat take your tongue?" I made no reply. The teacher asked again, "Did the cat take your tongue?" Again I made no reply. They laughed and continued to talk with the other children. I was embarrassed and felt unworthy of their attention. I wanted to be loved and accepted but I did not meet their approval. Approval was something I longed for all my life. Not meeting the approval of others was extremely devastating for me. The nursery rhyme of Humpty Dumpty explains well what happened to me when my actions did not meet the approval of others. Humpty Dumpty fell off the wall and all the king's horses and all the king's men could not put Humpty together again. I felt as though I could not be put together again. I was broken beyond repair.

Punishment Brought Shame

I was eleven years old and my brothers and I were to wash the eggs on a Sunday afternoon while our parents took a nap. It was a warm spring day and our grandparents came to our home to go for a walk. They asked us to join them to get some moist woods dirt for Grandma's violets. We had a great time walking along the creek and through the woods. Evening came and my brothers helped milk the cows. I was in the house doing the dishes. My dad came into the house and asked me if the eggs had been washed before we went on the walk. Only then did I realize I had made a huge mistake. I knew immediately that I had not met Dad's approval. He told me he had spanked my brothers out in the barn and he took me into the dining room. He asked me to lean over his knee and I received the first spanking I ever remember getting. I do not recall the physical pain, but the shame of being spanked was enormous. I was angry, humiliated and disgraced. I knew I had done wrong, but believed the punishment to be unjustified. In my fixation upon this humiliating experience I wanted to punish my dad. It was unthinkable to talk back so I devised another plan. I chose not to pray for him. I do not know how long I carried out my plan, but the results were long lasting. The shame of the spanking built a wall between my dad and myself. I carried that shame for many years. My head knew I was loved, but my heart was not sure.

I found healing from that experience after I was a parent. I had surgery and as a result I could not care for our six-month-old daughter. My parents had brought her over to see Les and me. It was winter and my dad was putting on Heidi's snowsuit. With the love and tenderness of a grandpa he was holding her in his arms. My heart broke as I wished I could be a little girl again and be held in my dad's arms. I wanted that love, but felt too ashamed to ask for it. I did not deserve his love. The next day I pulled together all the courage I could manage and asked my dad to come over because I had something I needed to share with him. As we sat on the sofa I shared my feelings about the spanking I had received. Dad did not remember the incident, but listened carefully as I poured out my hurts to him. I told him of the wall I had felt between us for these many years. I asked his forgiveness for not praying for him. He asked my forgiveness for spanking me at an age that was not appropriate. We held each other and cried. I was forgiven and the shame was removed. Today my dad is one of my greatest supporters and I know in both my heart and head that he loves me.

Laws Brought Shame

As a child I had a tender heart toward God. My mother would read us Bible stories and the story of the crucifixion touched me so deeply that I cried. I wanted to become a Christian and ask Jesus into my heart. I struggled because that would mean I was expected to wear a prayer veil on my head. I did not want to be different or be teased. The feeling of shame had caused me to close my heart to God as a young child. Each year during revival meetings I said no to becoming a Christian. One summer there was a tent meeting and the preacher asked all who knew they would go to heaven if Jesus came back tonight to stand. He told those of us who were sitting that we would go to hell. The struggle concerning wearing the prayer veil to school appeared insignificant when I thought of spending eternity in hell.

Adolescent Shame

My adolescent years carried many mixed feelings, which included my struggle with shame. The worm of shame slithered through my soul. My brothers began to date and I was excluded from that experience. I had gotten heavy, had acne and believed I was ugly. I had dreamed of being able to date as my brothers did, but it was only a dream. My mother would sew me a new dress for the school social, but I was never asked. I stood along the wall with the other dateless girls and we were paired with the boys who could not find dates or did not have the courage to ask a girl to the social. If there were not enough boys to go around we were paired with another girl for the games. One rainy day as I was walking to class, a popular guy came up to me and began talking.

I asked if he would like to walk under my umbrella. He accepted my offer and we walked to the next class together. A friend saw him and made a remark signifying that he was "scraping the bottom of the barrel" to walk with me. This young man's remark pained me and again I became a worm crawling around on my belly.

For the young people in my community, a popular activity after church on a Sunday evening was to drive around Joe Meyer's Diner. It was wrong to spend money on Sunday, but it was acceptable to check out the guys that were parked at the diner. I had never participated in this activity and was glad when asked by some younger girls if I would drive them around. They knew some of the guys and got excited. Even though I was driving I felt used as a means to an end, not included as a friend. I was a misfit and was never asked again.

When I was young, in the Mennonite church, we practiced foot washing before the sacrament of communion. I dreaded the foot washing practice because we would pair up with a friend. There were three of us girls about the same age and I was the odd one. I was left to find another "odd female" with whom I could wash feet. I felt unacceptable and not part of the group. The foot washing ceremony was to express our willingness to be a servant to others. Instead of experiencing servant-hood I experienced exclusiveness and shame.

As a young adult I left the Mennonite church and was thankful I left behind the experience of foot washing. I had concluded it was outdated and had no positive meaning for me. Some years after my marriage I returned to the Mennonite faith and I had opportunity to participate in the practice of foot washing. The gathering was rather small and Ada Marie asked if she could wash my feet. She knelt by the basin and washed my feet with her work worn hands. Then, ever so gently she dried my feet with the towel. I did the same for her. We embraced and wished each other the blessing of the Lord. That evening Ada Marie did more than wash my feet, she accepted me and included me in the family of God. It was a most holy moment when the shame connected with foot washing was banished. Several months later, Ada Marie fell while washing windows and died. I am thankful for the precious gift she gave to me before she left this earth. I felt chosen.

Usually, the church did not give me the feeling of being chosen. I felt it was shameful to be a female. I was second-class and unworthy of being spoken to by God. I remember being at a conference searching for more of God. I was lying in the grass on my belly arguing with God about opening my life to a fuller expression of His presence. I was fearful God would ask me to do something that would bring even more shame upon me. I would become more of a misfit because nobody would understand God's power in my life.

Later I had a very meaningful experience with God when I visited my cousin at college. I felt God's closeness and acceptance of me as a person whom He loved as I knelt at the altar. A feeling of joy and new openness to God in my life consumed my innermost being. No longer did I feel shameful before God. I willingly surrendered to Him. I shared this with my youth pastor and he discounted it as an emotional experience that was not valid and would soon become unimportant to me. I had taken the risk to share with my pastor an experience and in turn I felt as though he discounted my relationship with God.

Female Shame

This has been a frequent experience for me as I relate to the male leaders in my church. I share from my heart issues that I believe God is revealing to me. The board nods their heads, give assent, but nothing is done. I wonder, if I were a male, would I get more action, or would it only be a nod of the head? Does being a female in the church give you a second-class position? Does God speak only to and through males? Is it shameful to be a female? Ever since I was a teenager, I felt God was calling me into ministry. The only possible way I could see this happening was by becoming the wife of a pastor. I attended bible school hoping to find a husband. I was unsuccessful so I decided to enter the field of nursing. When I met Les and we married I had a question that kept haunting me. Did I misread the Spirit speaking to me as a teenager or did I make a mistake by marrying Les? I was torn and troubled by that question. Many times I felt angry because I was not born a male.

It has only been within the last year that I've realized God has called me, and not another. My experiences in Clinical Pastoral Education have opened new opportunities for me. I have been empowered and encouraged to own God's call on my life. As I realize what this experience means, I am able to move beyond the shame of being a female that caused life to be drained from me. I have been impregnated with a new life—the life of the Spirit.

Fear and shame have been the twins I have carried in my womb. I have held shame in relationship to sexuality. When I was dating a guy in Philadelphia, he became more aggressive than was comfortable for me. I was frightened because the last relationship he had been in was with a forty-year-old woman. In the midst of my fear I drove him home since he did not have a car. When I shared this experience with my female roommate she told me that as long as I didn't have intercourse it was okay. Then she commented that I would never make a man happy. I heard her saying that my fear of what happened on my date meant that I would never be able to make a man happy. This has been a tape that plays through my head more often than I want to admit. When I met Les, I carried that baggage with me. As we were dating I had high standards and had to tell Les no.

Then the tape would begin to play, "You'll never be able to make a man happy." The first night of our honeymoon was disappointing for both of us. Out of Les' pain he began to share his activities with a previous girlfriend. I felt humiliated and discounted as his wife. I was a failure and wanted to run away and hide. In my need to please, I felt abused and raped.

As our years of marriage progressed I became more and more distant emotionally and physically from my husband. I would sleep way over on my side of the bed and try not to touch him. If our bodies made contact with each other it meant sex. I was a turtle and pulled myself into my shell. Heidi was born a year and a half after we were married. She was a very fussy, colicky baby and I spent many hours pushing her in the stroller through the house trying to get her to sleep. Finally she would settle and I would ever so quietly slip into bed. If Les woke up he would want sex. I felt used only to meet his physical needs. I told God it would be fine with me if he had a mistress. I was willing to meet the rest of his needs. Sex held no pleasure for me. Sex brought physical pain and emotional shame. With my need to please, I continued to feel abused and raped. I was glad when I had physical problems that relieved me from my sexual responsibility. I felt as though I had married an untamable animal. He became much like the wolf in "Little Red Riding Hood." He was to be feared because he was lurking behind every tree ready to grab and devour me.

I never shared my fears or feeling of inadequacy with Les. The message he gave me was that he wanted sex more often and my body language said stay away from me. After ten years of marriage I could no longer carry my heavy box of hurts. I told my parents that my marriage was killing me. I did not know which way to turn. They were shocked because they had no idea of my struggles. I had hidden it so well. Several months later Les and I went to Recovery of Hope, a program for hurting marriages. We were put on the waiting list and during that time I slept on the sofa. Les wanted to talk about what I thought the problem was with our marriage. In his eyes our marriage was fine. I refused to speak to the issue because I also did not know what the problem was. All I knew was that I was not happy and had a terrible heaviness that I could no longer handle. When we were out in public we put on our happy face and tried to act as though everything was fine. Wearing a mask was the only means I had of coping.

In searching for an understanding of my shame of sex I attempted to share it with a therapist and even my pastor and his wife. The only result was that more shame was heaped upon me. Through the C.P.E. program I have been able to be in touch with my feelings and discover the source of my fears and shame. This has become a healing experience for me.

Understanding Shame

My understanding of shame began when I read *Shame; A Faith Perspective*, by Robert H. Albers, PhD. As I was reading I kept saying, "This is me. This is me." Albers' writings gave words to the feelings I had lived with for most of my life. I now had available some useful tools. My first attempt to use these tools was facing the shame of illness. Because I have been healthy the last two years, this was rather easy to deal with. A much more painful experience happened during C.P.E. class time. I had shared a verbatim that involved my relationship with a gay couple. During this presentation I shared fears, pain and uncertainty concerning homosexuality. I felt as if I had stripped myself naked before my peers. The group and leaders did not attend to me; rather I was feeling embarrassed, while they focused on an issue brought up by another peer. I had been vulnerable with my peers and instead of understanding I received shame. Another experience I had in the class setting was when I was accused of not being understanding of racial situations. They pointed their fingers at me and questioned my integrity. In both of these situations I was overcome with shame and knew what was happening to my soul. After discussing the situations with Urias I was able to confront those involved and share my feelings. This was a giant step toward wholeness for me.

As I noted earlier my health has also been a source of shame for me. I was only twenty-six years old when a disc in my neck ruptured. I had surgery and then several months later I began having problems again, which required a cervical fusion. Then it was a hysterectomy and later a para-thyroidectomy. Lastly, another cervical fusion. I was angry because I had lost control over my body. Nobody else in my family has the struggles with their health that I have experienced. Am I not worthy of good health? When I had my first neck surgery a woman in the church told me that if I would remove my cervical brace God would heal my neck. I was afraid to follow her command and then shame fell upon me. I was ashamed that I did not have enough faith to remove the brace. If I had taken the brace off, would I have been healed? I do not know and it will always remain a mystery for me.

Shame is part of our human condition and we will at times have it raise its ugly head and stare us in the face. If we recognize shame for what it is, a condition of fallen humanity, it will lose its control over us. A turning point comes for us as we change our point of focus from shame to the healing power of God. The result is peace and contentment with others and ourselves.

Reflection from Sara

When I think of the shame of illness, I remember the woman Jesus healed of her hemorrhaging condition, whom we read about in Mark 5:25-34. She had suffered with this bleeding problem for twelve years and had been to many doctors. The worst of it was that she could not go to the temple for worship because she was considered unclean. She had heard that Jesus healed others so she decided to go to Him for healing. There was no way she would speak to Him about her problem so she said to herself that if she could just touch His clothing, she would be healed. I can only imagine her great joy when she touched the back of His cloak and she felt her bleeding stop. But, then Jesus asked who had touched Him. Of course He knew! This woman needed more than physical healing. Her disease had heaped shame upon her. She mustered all the courage she had within her being and announced to all that she was the one who had touched Jesus. She fell at His feet, trembling with fear, telling Him the whole truth. She went away in peace, freed from her suffering, experiencing healing from shame.

We find the story of another woman's relationship with Jesus in Luke 7:36-50. This woman had lived a sinful life. She had heard that Jesus was eating at Simon's house. She brought with her an alabaster jar of perfume. This woman began to weep, and as she wept, her tears wet His feet. Her grief and sorrow must have been overwhelming to cause enough tears to wet the feet of Jesus. After the tears ended she dried His feet with her hair and then poured the perfume on them.

Those gathered around could not believe that Jesus was allowing a sinful woman to minister to Him. Jesus' response to the people was that those who have experienced forgiveness respond in love to the one who has forgiven them.

My response to this story was to lie on the floor and weep before God, asking Him to forgive me for the times I allowed fear and shame to control my actions. This story took on a new and fresh meaning. I realized that if I would have been that woman, I would have been too fearful of what others thought to express my love to Jesus. My healing has been a two-year process as I've kept my heart open to the working of the Spirit in my life. When I feel God's healing touch, I experience a trembling of my body, not from fear, but from the presence of the Spirit.

Reflection from Lori

For me, the ultimate experience of shame in the Bible is the crucifixion of Jesus. The movie, *The Passion of the Christ,* has brought this event to life for all to see the humiliation and shame that Jesus endured as He hung on the cross. As I reflect on the words that I wrote about my shame, "I will not carry it for them any longer. I am free," I wonder if Jesus thought these same things as He was beaten and spit upon. He carried the shame of our sin through His arrest and the painful, humiliating scourging. I don't know if I could withstand the physical pain of taking the punishment for someone I love, but He did. At the moment of His death, before the final breath was released from His body, Jesus freed us from the sin and shame of this world. He had won our forgiveness by being obedient to God. And, God rewarded Him with eternal life of peace and joy. I have also been rewarded for being obedient to God. He has given me freedom from my past and the strength to move forward. He has also given me the gift to sit with others in their pain and suffering. The wounds that shame had caused have created a deep sensitivity within me toward those who are experiencing hurt, disappointment and anger in their lives. Jesus has endless compassion for those in pain. Whatever we feel, He has already felt. Every experience we have, He has already had. When someone hurts us, He feels the pain, too. The shame and sin that Jesus carried to the cross has been replaced with tender love as He now carries us to freedom. I can imagine Him saying, "I will always carry them. Because of our Father, we are all free."

Fuel for your journey

1. Which story caused you to think of your own experiences? Why?

2. How does it make you feel?

3. What would you like to say to God right now?

4. Who can you share these feelings with?

CHAPTER FOUR

Change
The Reality of Life

Nature gives us a beautiful picture of change. The miracle of change is demonstrated for us in the metamorphosis of the caterpillar. A furry multi-legged worm crawls on the ground. This creature becomes hungry and begins to feast upon the fresh green leaves of plants. After it has stuffed itself to the greatest capacity possible, it begins to make a chrysalis. For several weeks, changes to the caterpillar are happening. However, these changes are hidden and cannot be observed.

It is necessary for the butterfly to beat its wings inside the chrysalis in order to gain enough strength to break through. At the appropriate time, the butterfly begins to emerge. It is motionless for several hours to allow time for its wings to dry. As they dry they become larger and larger. The fibers of the wings become strong enough so the butterfly can begin to fly.

No longer does this creature crawl on its belly. The change has brought new possibilities, which will soon become limitless. The beauty of the wings is the work of a masterful artist. They are delicate, but so very strong. The butterfly, seemingly without effort, glides into space, knowing a freedom it never experienced as a caterpillar.

The butterfly has been a symbol for us of the change that we have experienced in our lives. At times the change is happening inside of us and nobody realizes what is taking place. Other times the change is very evident and family and friends take notice. Change is God's gift to us even though it often is accompanied by fear and pain. Sometimes, this transition into something new is out of our control and we become angry. But, with every change, God is waiting for us to open our hearts to the Grace of possibilities that are before us. Each time we are faced with a new beginning, we have learned how important it is to grieve the loss of what is ending. When God closes one door, it's vital that we let the door close completely, before moving through the one He has opened. Along the way, we will take the wisdom we have gained from our experience of change. Most importantly, we need to say good-bye, before we can say hello.

Sara

A Fact of Life

Change is a fact of life. From the moment of our conception until our time of death, we change. We have the choice of embracing and working with change or fearing and fighting the change. The choice is ours.

Breaking the chains of fear and shame has brought a huge change into my life. First it was necessary for me to realize that I was bound and limited by my chains. There was no freedom of the spirit. I longed to live in freedom so I attempted to pull free of the chains until my hands and feet were bleeding. All my efforts were to no avail. I needed someone with the key to release me. I knew Jesus had the key, so I cried out to Him for help. He then sent me human instruments to turn the key and I was free.

My freedom has come at a price. It was imperative that I be willing to look at my chains. Closing my eyes and being very still would not make them disappear. These chains were as real as if they had been made of iron. They were cold, hard and brought no comfort to my soul. I tried to hide my chains from others, but they were out in the open for all to see. The fact that chains bound me was shameful. The chains were real and not a figment of my imagination. I needed to acknowledge my imprisonment. I was not perfect. I was bound! All the pride in the world could not loosen my chains. I faced my humanity, looked and touched my chains. Then held out my hands and feet as the key was turned.

I'm exploring my new freedom. I have changed from the fearful, unworthy person to a woman of enthusiasm and power. When I read this scripture in Acts 1:8,

> *"But you will receive power when the Holy*
> *Spirit comes upon you; and you will be my wit-*
> *nesses in Jerusalem, and in all Judea and*
> *Samaria, and to the ends of the earth."*

I wondered when I would know the power from the Holy Spirit that Jesus had promised before He ascended into heaven. Since the chains of fear and shame no longer bind me, I have experienced the power of which He spoke. There is a new energy and vitality in my spirit. I speak and move with authority and power—not my own, but one given to me as a gift from God. When bound by chains, I could neither use nor explore the gift God wanted to give to me. As I got rid of the chains the wounds around my ankles and wrists began to heal. The scars will remain to remind me of the freedom that is now mine.

Step by Step

God is wise in bringing change into our lives on the installment basis. Sometimes we begin with only baby steps. Other times we turn a deaf ear to His voice of guidance. This is what happened to me when I left my nursing position. I had been feeling a nudge from God to become a chaplain, but nursing provided financial security. I felt needed and was told I was irreplaceable in the office. I did not have the courage to acknowledge what I believed God was asking of me. I continued to work in the office and then my body was affected. I ruptured two discs in my neck. After the surgery I did not recover as I had hoped. God had my full attention when I was flat on my back. Because I was unable to contribute toward our financial needs for more than a year, we learned that we could live within Les' income.

During those months God continued to give me the desire to pursue chaplaincy. I chose to enroll in a sixteen-week class, planning to go back to my hometown and work as a chaplain in the local nursing homes. God's dreams were bigger than I had ever envisioned. He opened the doors for me to do a chaplain residency at Covenant HealthCare and gave me the desire to become a certified chaplain. At the age of fifty-five I will begin working toward a Master of Divinity degree. This will bring many changes for my husband and me. So I can attend seminary, we plan to move from what we thought would become our dream retirement home by the lake. Even though these changes are exciting and I look upon them as a time of adventure, there is also a certain amount of fear because I'm moving into an unknown academic world. I've never attended college, but I have an opportunity to study for a masters degree. At times I see myself as a butterfly experiencing the freedom that comes with the development of wings and on other occasions I feel like I'm still in the chrysalis flapping my wings, trying to make them strong enough to fly.

Some changes we make in our life are just matter of fact and we handle them with ease. Others bring struggle and cause us pain. The first time I left my daughters with a babysitter that was not family was difficult for me. It was only for several hours while I did some housecleaning for a friend. I was surprised when my eyes filled with tears and my voice was crackly and gruff as I told them good-bye. I felt silly to be reacting in this manner. After several weeks I had accepted the change and could leave without feelings of guilt and sorrow. I experienced these feelings to a much greater degree when our older daughter left home after high school. Going to visit her for the first time was almost as traumatic as watching her leave for Pennsylvania at five o'clock in the morning. I was not ready to see my child become independent of me. In my head I knew this was what I had been training her for these last eighteen years, but my mother's heart was screaming inside that I was not ready. When our second daughter left home it was not as difficult for me, because I knew I would survive the pain of separation and change. This was part of allowing my children to become whole and complete without me. They will always be held close to my heart, but they have become their own persons and free to make their own choices.

Change Is a Choice

The freedom of choice is a valuable gift that we give to others as well as to ourselves. After ten years of marriage I was ready to leave my husband because the relationship was taking too much energy. I thought there were no options and no other way out of my distress. While we were receiving therapy at Recovery of Hope, I learned that other options were available.

I chose to change the way I viewed my husband. No longer did I focus on his weaknesses, rather I chose to also look at his strengths. He is great at fixing anything that needs to be repaired, he keeps the car in excellent working condition, and there are many activities we enjoy doing together. He is not perfect, but neither am I. It is amazing how much the mind controls our ability to change. One of the agreements of our marriage contract as we concluded our week of intensive therapy was that I would read a romance novel once a month. This would help to get my mind into the romantic mode. Several times Les has asked me, "When was the last time you read a romance book?" I get the hint and make a trip to the library. This is a huge change for me to be able to joke and laugh about my lack or low level of romantic feelings. We have now been married thirty years and our marriage relationship has become more light-hearted and fun.

As I reflect upon our move from Pennsylvania to Michigan I perceive it as preparing us for a walk of faith. Making the choice to follow the leading of the Spirit, even though in many ways it did not make sense, was a risk. I gave up a job at a large Christian bookstore, which I enjoyed. Les accepted a job that provided only half the income he had earned previously. Because real estate prices were lower, we were able to purchase a home without a mortgage. As we moved with the Spirit one step at a time God blessed us and affirmed our decision to move from family and friends to an unknown land.

It took me five years to call Pigeon, Michigan, home. I missed my support system of friends. While Les went to work and the girls to school, I stayed home and removed old brick chimneys, painted rough plaster walls, and scraped off ancient wallpaper. My role had changed and it was difficult to accept. I had made new friends, but I still felt lonely. In my loneliness, I reached out to God, and after the house was remodeled, I had an opportunity to return to a nursing career that I had left for more than fifteen years.

With change comes a growing edge. As Lori and I begin writing each chapter of the book we joke and tell each other that this chapter will be easier than the last. In our hearts we know that God is going to use each topic to bring growth into our lives. And growth means change. As I've said, the C.P.E. program has been extremely instrumental in my life. God has used this environment to produce growth and to refine my skills.

As I write this chapter God is bringing more change into my life. The Spirit of God is asking me to leave the C.P.E. program and take the summer off to write this book. My fellow students have become my family and I don't want to leave, but the other part of me is saying you must follow the leading of the Spirit. How do I work through these questions and feelings? I found a book that I had read for class very helpful, *The Minister as Diagnostician*, by Paul W. Pruyser. He uses the following seven guidelines of diagnosis and I worked through these to help me make a decision:

(1) *What is most important to me?* In my heart of hearts it is most important for me to listen and obey the leading of the Spirit.

(2) *Is there any divine purpose in my situation?* God has called me to bring a message of hope to many through my writing.

(3) *Does my faith open or close me to new opportunities?* As I move in faith God is providing new opportunities of growth and ministry.

(4) *Have I experienced God's grace as he smiles at me?* At this moment I see God with a broad grin giving me a "thumbs up."

(5) *Is my heart open to move beyond remorse to repentance?*
My desire is as the psalmist says in *Psalms 139:23-24;*

> *"Search me, O God, and know my heart; try*
> *me, and know my anxieties; and see if there is*
> *any wicked way in me, and lead me in the way*
> *everlasting."*

(6) *Am I able to connect with humanity?* In my writing I have
shared with an open honest heart in the hope of connecting with others on their journey.

(7) *Do I have a sense of purpose that will move the world*
towards integrity? My purpose is to guide others to find
their own hope and healing in life and become a person
of enthusiasm.

Through looking at these questions I have found my
answer. The Spirit has stirred the waters and there is more
change on the horizon.

When we control or initiate the change that enters our
life, we have a certain type of feeling. When change is forced
upon us as a result of another's choice, change can become
much more difficult. Most of the changes I have experienced
in my life have been my own. Sometimes they may not have
been the wisest or the best, but they were choices I made and I
accepted ownership of those decisions.

As I evaluate and analyze my reaction to the changes in my
life, the bottom line is that of control. Even though I may find
the change difficult, I can still maintain my identity and power
if I make the choice to change. So even though I feel as if God is
pushing me out of the boat and asking me to swim, I still have
the choice of hanging onto the boat and not allowing myself to
be pushed into the water or jumping into the water and learning to swim. The choice to accept change, or not, is mine.

Lori
Change of Spirit

When a woman reaches a certain age and begins menopause, we call it "going through the change." This is very true, since our bodies are being transformed into something different than they were when we were young. All kinds of feelings are stirred up during this time. Grief at losing our youth, elation at not having to deal with periods anymore, sadness that we can no longer bear children and fear of who we will be on the other side of "the change." This physical change of our bodies is expected and accepted. People usually understand and even joke about it. It's a fact of life. But what happens when someone goes through a spiritual change of life? Or how do others react when a person makes changes in their life that they do not agree with? Will there be compassion and support?

These are a few of the questions I have been asking myself for a long time now. Unfortunately, I haven't found the answers I was hoping for. The control that my parents and siblings have had in my life finally became unbearable for me. I felt like I was suffocating. I couldn't make any decisions on my own without consulting them first. It wasn't that they always demanded it, but it was the only way I knew. I can't recall exactly when I started to pull away from their grip, but I do remember how difficult it was. The change began slowly and subtly with things like deciding not to go to all of the family reunions and parties or not going to my parent's house every week. Each time Duane and I made these decisions, my mom would get mad and try to make me feel guilty. At first, this tactic worked on me, but eventually I began to let the guilt go. This process took many years for me to go through. I can't count how many times I slid back under their control before finally breaking free of it.

I have learned that change is very frightening for some people. The fear is so great that even when the opportunity for growth and a better life would be the result of a change, they resist because of the possibility of failure. These are the people that have to be in control of everything in their lives and when they are not, they dig in their heels and hold on as tight as they can to the way life has always been. And, then there are those that know they would have to honestly look at themselves and all of their sins in order to begin to change who they are. When someone close to them begins to change, especially if it involves a spiritual conversion, it is threatening because it may upset the balance in their lives.

Growing Pains

This is what happened in my family. My parents and siblings are so stuck in the fallacy of a perfect family that when they realized I was moving out from their control, they became cruel, opinionated and rigid. I have become the problem in the family. As long as they can keep the focus on me, they can retain some sort of control and be able to justify how they have treated me.

I'm sure that watching me change and grow is scary for my parents. I wonder how many times they have worried that the secret of abuse would be revealed if I became strong enough and independent of them. In some ways, I feel sorry for them. They must have known that this would happen some day, which would explain why they were not supportive of my education at the Diocese. When I was first accepted into the program, they seemed to be happy about it. I started noticing a change within just a few months after my classes began.

The Lay Ministry Program is a four-year process to becoming a commissioned lay minister. During the first two years we met for classes one weekend every month. In between, there were assignments to complete, reading to prepare for the next class and papers to write. The final two years, our class was together twice each year to reflect on our ministries and to prepare to be commissioned by the bishop. This became an amazing time in my life, even with the intensity of working full time, raising a family and going to classes. I found that I really enjoyed learning and I was hungry to learn as much as I could about God. This education just felt right to me, it felt good to be doing this for myself and I had found a place that I belonged. No one judged me. I felt comfortable and accepted for who I was. I was very excited about my future and my relationship with God.

A few weeks before classes began, we gathered for an orientation evening. The directors of the program told us about the curriculum and how much time would be needed for studying. They suggested that we share this with our families so they would understand that our time was going to be very limited for a couple of years. Duane and the kids were very supportive and told me that they would do whatever they could to help out. I also explained to the rest of the family that I was going to be very busy and that it wasn't that I didn't want to spend time with them, but that this was a very important priority in my life right now. I thought they understood.

Things began okay, but quickly I began getting phone calls from my mom telling me that I never spent any time with her anymore. I explained over and over again, but this complaint went on for months. I tried to find time that I could be with her by inviting her to go to mass with me. She said she would but it never happened. There were also some very interesting classes about the sacraments in the program that I invited her to come with me as my guest, but that didn't work either. She became very demanding of my time, even though during the first two years I never missed any holidays or birthdays with the family. It seemed that no matter what I did, I was always in trouble so I started backing away from her. When this happened and she began losing her control over me, the arguments started. Then the rest of the family joined her in accusing me of not wanting to be with them anymore. They had come to this conclusion from what Mom was telling them and not from talking to me. I remember a phone call from one of my brothers one night in which he told me, "If what you are doing is causing you to sacrifice the family, then you have to quit." My response was a firm no. I didn't feel that I was sacrificing them, I felt and still feel that they have sacrificed me.

The conflict with the family continued over the next two years. During this time I began to move farther and farther away from their control. The change that occurred in me was that I could now see the dysfunction within this family. I was far enough away to be able to look at it more objectively and to realize that the things I had always thought of as normal were definitely not. At this distance, I began to find my strength to stand on my own and to use my own voice. This strength has contributed to a very drastic change in my relationship with the family. During a phone call from my mom one night, about a year ago, in which she accused me of something I did not do, I surprised her by standing up for myself. I quietly explained that I was not at fault in this situation. She continued to yell at me and I continued to say that I did nothing wrong. Not knowing how to respond, she hung up quickly and there has been no contact with the family since. My sister has called occasionally, but she's not able to understand that I will not apologize for something I didn't do. There have been no holidays or birthdays with the family and my kids have been pushed away as well.

I realize now that I needed to make the break and move away in order to become aware of the secrets of my past. As long as they controlled me, my mind protected me from remembering the abuse. But, God had other plans. He knew that the secret had to be revealed and I was the one to do it. In order for me to become strong enough to accept what had happened to me as a child, God needed to bring me back to Him. He needed to change the belief I had that He didn't know me or care about me. That change had already begun when I met Duane, but my heart was still reluctant. And, then God gave me a very precious gift. In the spring of 1988 He arranged for Margaret to enter my life.

Pearls of Wisdom

I will never forget the day we met. I had just started my job at the hospital gift shop where Margaret was a volunteer. It was the third day of my training and I had met many new people in those few days. They were all very nice and I felt welcome and comfortable in this new position. Since there were so many to remember I was very grateful that everyone wore ID badges with their first names on them. So that morning when another volunteer arrived and I was introduced to her, I was a little intimidated by her when I read her name tag. It said "Mrs. R. Schoen." It seemed to me that this volunteer was one that demanded respect. I wasn't sure how I should address her. Then she shook my hand and with a sweet smile, said, "It's so nice to meet you, dear. Please call me Margaret." In that moment, my first impression of her melted away and I knew that we would be friends.

Margaret and I learned a lot about each other in a short time. She was almost seventy-five years old and had been volunteering at the gift shop for about fifteen years. Her hair was the most beautiful shade of white and her blue eyes sparkled as we shared our stories. She was very petite, about 5'2", but for some reason she seemed very tall to me. I guess it was because I looked "up" to her. I began to look forward to the times that we would work together in the gift shop. As our relationship grew, she told me about her husband, Bob. By this time, he had been gone for more than twenty-five years. They had not been able to have children and she still missed him very much. Whenever she talked about him, her eyes filled with tears. She still felt married to him, which is why her name tag said what it did. He was and always would be her husband. Margaret was a very strong and independent woman. She lived alone, took care of her own finances and always drove a Cadillac. I admired her so much. Within a few months Margaret had become part of our family and my mentor.

During our ten years together we shared a lot of laughter and many tears. But, our last year was the most precious of all. At the age of eighty-five she was diagnosed with uterine cancer. The doctors wanted to begin radiation and chemotherapy immediately, but Margaret was hesitant. She wanted time to think about it. Over the next few days we discussed her options many times. I assured her that whatever decision she made, I would accept it and be with her every step of the way. Finally, she decided that she would not take the treatment, but rather enjoy whatever time she had left for as long as she could. Margaret felt that she had lived a long, happy life and now it was time to get ready to see her beloved Bob once again.

I didn't want to lose her, but I supported her decision as I had promised her I would. My greatest concern was that she not suffer any pain. Margaret had become so very important in my life. She had shown me unconditional love and I had thrived on it. Her faith in God was strong, yet she never pushed me to accept Him into my life. She lived what she believed and was a wonderful example to me of God's love. My love for her was so great that I decided to try to pray for her. I was sure that God knew her and maybe He would hear my prayers because of her. So I prayed, day and night, asking only that Margaret would not have any pain. In the beginning I didn't know if He was hearing me, but I didn't give up. It was the only way I knew of helping her.

Eventually, Margaret's condition worsened and she became bedridden. Even as her health deteriorated, her spirit remained alive. Her eyes still sparkled every time I visited. During this time I began to realize that she was not having any pain from the cancer. She had a tumor that was protruding from her abdomen and endless fatigue, but she remained free of pain. I was very grateful, yet astounded that God had heard my prayers. I began to wonder if maybe, just maybe, He did know me. Slowly, I began to make that transition into believing that God was there for me and had been all the time.

Shortly before Margaret died, I began to panic. I could not imagine my life without her. She was always there when I needed her. She listened to me, encouraged me and held me when I cried. Under her tender care, I had been nurtured and protected with a mother's love. I had longed for this my whole life and now it was going to be gone. In the midst of my grief, I started to hear a voice. At first I pushed it away, but it became stronger and stronger until at last I surrendered and listened. It was God's voice telling me that I could now run to Him. His arms were open wide and waiting for me. He would nurture and protect me and He would provide me with unconditional love. I could no longer remember a time when He wasn't there for me. My tears of losing Margaret turned to tears of shame for having doubted God in the first place. This is what I had been longing for and Margaret had shown me the way.

A few weeks later, my beloved Margaret passed away peacefully in her sleep at home and without pain. It has been more than six years now and I still miss her deeply. I feel that I will always grieve her loss. But, my life has gone on and I believe that someday I will see her again because of what she taught me. God has blessed me for the pain of losing Margaret and having the courage to make this tremendous change in my life. He has helped me to find the strength I've needed to follow His plan for my life and I have continued to thrive. I have learned that every change in my life has opened my heart to the possibilities of His Grace in my life. Each time I come face to face with change, I need to remember to ask what God wants me to learn from this experience. The most important thing I've learned is that even though every change can be extremely painful, I know that I will survive it because of what Margaret taught me and because God is always with me.

Stand Straight; Stand Tall; Be Strong

My most recent struggle with change began just as I was preparing to write my stories for this chapter. I was given a referral from the night chaplain as I arrived for report, to check on the family of a fifteen-year-old boy who had been in a very serious car accident. As I walked the halls to the Pediatric Intensive Care Unit, my thoughts were focused on helping this family through their crisis. I had absolutely no idea that this family would help me to face another change in my life.

I had learned during morning report that the boy, Eddie, had been a passenger in a car that had rolled and came to rest upside down in a deep ditch filled with water. The driver was also brought to the hospital in critical condition. Both boys had been submerged in the water for more than ten minutes. There was little hope of recovery for either. The families had arrived and been given the prognosis by the doctors. Eddie's family had been told that he had suffered severe brain and lung damage. The chances for survival were very, very slim.

When I arrived on the unit, I felt the sense of heaviness that is always present on the floor when a child is near death. The staff was very solemn and quiet. They spoke in hushed voices as they told me of their concern for Eddie's family. The doctor filled me in on the latest test results and asked me to stay nearby. I remember thinking how grateful I was for my relationships with the PICU staff at that moment. It was important that we all be on the same page in order to provide the best care possible for the patient and his family.

After speaking with the staff, I went to see Eddie. What I saw made me incredibly sad. Lying in the hospital bed was a beautiful young man with long legs, dark wavy hair and the beginnings of a mustache coming in. There were tubes attached everywhere. The respirator was breathing for him and he was non-responsive. The nurse was watching the monitors and checking IVs. Then I saw a man standing by the window. He had the same dark hair as Eddie and he looked very tired. I introduced myself to him and learned that he was Eddie's dad. Within a few minutes I met his mom. This was the beginning of my twenty-nine hour relationship with an incredible family.

As the hours passed on our first day together, I learned a lot about Eddie. His family shared their love for him with me. I began to know each of them and was very impressed at their strength and compassion for each other. The results of every test the doctors ordered were not encouraging. Eddie's condition continued to deteriorate. The family made the decision to remove life support, but wished to wait until Eddie's older brother and sister could arrive from out of state. The doctors were hopeful that the machines could sustain his life for a few more hours. At the end of my shift, I said good-bye to Eddie and his family, certain that he would not survive the night. I passed my referral on to the night chaplain and went home.

I had a difficult time sleeping that night. I kept praying that Eddie wouldn't suffer any longer. I asked God to help Eddie's family find some hope from this tragedy and to give them strength to say good-bye to their child. The next morning, as I got ready for work, Eddie was still on my mind. There are times when patients touch me deeply and this was one of them. I was anxious to get to work to find out how things had progressed during the night.

When I arrived for report I was very surprised to hear that Eddie had survived the night. His siblings had arrived about four in the morning. It was now seven and the terminal wean was planned for late morning when more family could be present. I went directly to the unit and spoke with the family. I promised them that I would be there whenever they needed me. I then learned from the doctor that the Gift of Life organization had been notified about possible organ donation by this patient. I wondered if this could be the hope for the family that I had asked God for.

A few hours later it had been determined that Eddie was a good candidate for organ donation and the family had consented. They told me that they were very relieved to find something positive out of all of this. Somehow, Eddie would live on through others who would surely die also, if not for this wonderful gift. The Gift of Life team went to work finding recipients for Eddie's organs and arranging for transplant teams to come to our hospital to perform the surgery.

About two hours before the surgery was set to begin, it was determined that in order to achieve the best possible results for transplantation, the terminal wean would have to be done in the operating room. This meant that Eddie's family would not be able to be with him when he died. As I said, this family was incredible. When the doctors explained the situation, they quickly agreed that they would do whatever was necessary to ensure the success of the organ donation. Their sacrifice touched me to the core. I watched as they held each other and cried together. I wondered if I were in this same situation if I would be as strong as they were.

I stayed with the family as they comforted one another. After a few minutes, I went to sit with Eddie's mom. She was sitting quietly and seemed lost in thought. I could only imagine the memories that she would be recalling of her son. We sat in silence for a while and when she looked up at me, I reached out to hold her hand. I will never forget the pain in her eyes as she said to me, "I won't be able to be with him. He will be alone." In that moment God told me what He wanted me to do. I felt the familiar stirring in my gut that was urging me to say the words. "Connie, would you like me to be with Eddie?" She looked at me at first with amazement and then with gratefulness, said yes. We had connected on the level that God had wanted us to. We were both moms. Connie trusted that I could feel her pain and that I would comfort her son as she would. And I trusted God to help me to comfort her.

Fortunately, I have been in the operating room on a couple of previous occasions so I knew what to expect and what I needed to do to get ready. After talking to the Gift of Life team about Connie's request, they immediately agreed. I went to the women's locker room in the O.R. and changed into scrubs, all the while praying intensely for God to be there to help me through this. I was already exhausted from the nearly fourteen hours I had worked so far that day. I had been with many other people before, as they had died, but never a fifteen-year old boy. I wasn't so sure that I could do this. Then I felt it. God's presence came over me like a rush of warm water. I felt extremely peaceful and confident. The anxiety I had felt earlier had completely disappeared. Now I knew that I wasn't alone. God would be with me every step of the way. He would give me the strength and the words I needed to comfort the family and the staff during this incredibly difficult time. At that moment I knew that something had changed in me. I was now able to recognize the power of God immediately without questioning it. But, I didn't have time to reflect on this change, I had work to do.

When I returned to Eddie's room, the nurse was preparing him to be moved to the operating room. I stood nearby with the family as they said good-bye to him. I followed as the staff wheeled Eddie down the hall toward the elevator and away from his parents. About half way, I turned around and saw Eddie's dad standing in the middle of the hall with tears streaming down his face and waving good-bye. I held my hand out to him and invited him to come with us to the elevator. He took my hand and we continued on. When the door opened, he hugged me and thanked me for going with his son. As I stepped onto the elevator I promised to take good care of him, and the doors closed.

In the operating room, things moved very quickly. I stayed near Eddie and watched with fascination this group of people whose passion was to save lives when others suddenly ended. The time came to remove life support. I prayed that Eddie would not suffer. The doctor removed the breathing tube and I sat next to Eddie, very close to his head. I ran my hands through his thick, wavy hair and stroked his forehead. I watched as his long, dark eyelashes fluttered with each breath. There was no suffering and I thanked God. As his breathing became shallow, I talked to him, telling him that he was a good boy and his mom and dad loved him very much. When his heart stopped, I silently released him into God's hands. Tears filled my eyes and fell into the surgical mask I was wearing. Everyone in the room was completely silent. I felt incredibly humbled that I had walked this journey with Eddie, taking him right to heaven's door and watched as his spirit flew to Jesus. It was time for me to leave. Eddie's suffering was over, but it had only begun for his family and I wanted to comfort them now.

We all sat together and waited for the surgery to be over. When it was, I took them to see their son one last time. The organ donation was very successful and several people were somewhere waiting for their gift of life to come to them. The family was exhausted and weak from grief as they left the hospital. I still felt God's presence with me as strong as it had been before Eddie died. As I hugged his parents good-bye, I prayed that they could take some of that Presence with them. By this time, it was twelve-thirty in the morning and my twenty-nine hour relationship with the family had come to an end.

I drove home, went to bed, but didn't sleep too well. The next morning as I was getting ready for work I realized that even though God was still with me, I couldn't feel the intensity of His presence any longer. I felt empty and very lonely. I struggled through the next few days trying to make sense of all my feelings. When I told Sara how I felt, she understood and reminded me that I had been walking on holy ground and of course I would be sad when I could no longer feel it. But, there were others that didn't understand. How could I explain so they could, if I didn't have words to describe my experience? I wanted to shout to the world and share God's love, but I became frustrated when people attributed my strength to be in that operating room to an adrenaline rush.

A few days after Eddie's death, I was driving to work just as the sun was rising. It was so beautiful, with rainbows of colors everywhere. I kept glancing back and forth between the road and the sun and then I saw a perfectly vertical ray of light directly above the middle of the sun. There were clouds in the sky and it looked like the cloud above the sun had been sliced down the center and separated to let this ray come through. I was looking at it in amazement when I heard God's voice in my mind. His words were, "Stand straight; Stand tall; Be strong. You have done what I've asked you to do and I believe in you." This was the change in me that I had briefly noticed a few nights before, but had forgotten in my sadness. I had recognized His presence immediately and did what He wanted me to do and it shouldn't matter what anyone else thought about it. I can stand up and shout to the world about God's love for me and it's okay if some don't believe, because there will be others that will. I have struggled for so long with other's opinions of me. God believes in me and that's all that truly matters. Just as I had let Eddie go into God's arms, I have also surrendered the parts of me that need to change.

Eddie's parents had the courage to do what they believed in, despite the sacrifice it required. They stood straight and tall. They were strong with God's presence. Their example has helped me to take another step in my journey. I can now see that I had been walking on holy ground for the entire twenty-nine hours with Eddie and his family. As painful as this experience was for me, this was the one that God placed before me as I started to write this chapter on change. I am grateful for it because now I feel free to share the power of God in my life and the resulting change in me. It's amazing to me that this change God had planned in me occurred as I was changing out of my clothes and into scrubs. I was putting on something that was new to me. It was as if I was trying on a new identity. For a few hours I was in a different world. I was in the world of medicine and technology. My uniform matched all the others in the operating room. We all looked the same. It was hard to tell who were doctors and who were nurses. There I was in a strange world and not quite fitting in. On the outside I looked the same as the others, but on the inside I was still me. What I realize now is that whatever a person looks like on the outside, whatever uniform they wear does not let us know who they really are. And, whatever uniform I may put on, it will never change my heart and what I believe in. God was showing me that I didn't need my chaplain coat or badge to be His instrument of comfort. The others in the room knew who I was because they saw my compassion and love for Eddie. I brought God into the operating room and His light shined through me. This is a major change for me because until now I thought that I needed the title of chaplain, in order to help people, but God has other plans for me. All I have to do is be myself, put on whatever uniform He requires and follow Him. But this change is difficult for me and it hurts, because for so long all I've wanted to be is a chaplain and now I'm hearing the call to surrender this identity to God in order to move on through the next door. So the question I have to ask myself is how important the title of chaplain is to my identity as a child of God? After some deep reflection I hope that I will have found some answers to share in the next chapter.

Struggles

Sara and I are realizing that each time we prepare to write the next chapter in our book, God has a surprise for us. As we faced fear, some fears that we thought we had moved away from resurfaced again with a vengeance. We both faced days of being submerged in fear once again. As we fought our way through it and began to write our stories, we realized that these were the issues that God wanted us to talk about. And in the freshness of our pain, we did. When the chapter was completed, we were elated. Now we knew what God wanted, we had to dig deep into our souls and share our pain. Good. We were ready to concentrate on shame. The stories that we came up with were good, but not good enough. Once again, God brought our shame and placed it directly in front of us. We couldn't run from it. We couldn't look the other way. We struggled and we cried. And then we wrote. From the struggle we arrived at a new level of understanding of ourselves and of each other. It was such a relief to have the chapter completed.

Having defeated our deepest fears and shame, we thought the worst was over. The next chapters would be much easier for us. Yet, here we are at change, and we are both facing difficult issues again. From the beginning, we knew that this book belongs to God and He was asking us to surrender our experiences to Him in order to help others. So, despite the difficulties we are facing, we are rejoicing in the possibilities in which

God will take our stories and use them to change people's lives. In the process, He is continuing to change our lives as well. We can't even imagine what He has planned for us when this book is complete. However, we are certain that He will offer us the gift of change, comfort us as we struggle through it and shower us with His Grace.

My daughter, Krystina, is also facing her struggles with change. This is her last year of high school and graduation is coming soon. She has been so ready for this part of her education to be done. However, the excitement she has felt has been replaced with sadness in these last few days of school. In her words, "It's all catching up to me." She is in transition. The door behind her is still open a crack, while the view through the door to her future is bright with wonder and possibilities. So the sadness has taken her by surprise. It's hard to realize that the people that have been part of her life for so long will no longer be there from day to day.

This is the reason we have ceremonies, rituals and traditions. Among the preparations for celebration, the school also plans for closure. "Senior Send Off" is one of those occasions. The entire high school staff and students gathered in the gym to say good-bye to the seniors that are leaving and welcome the juniors taking their place in the fall. Beginnings and endings. Coming and going. Saying good-bye and saying hello. Graduation and commencement. These are our rituals.

This transition will pass for Krystina as she eases into her future. The sadness that she feels today will be replaced with happy memories and confidence in knowing she'll be able to face the next change in her life, whatever that may be. She will learn that it's okay to cry and laugh at the same time. She will realize as that door finally closes, that what she has learned from this experience will carry her through the open door. It's part of change. It's part of life. It's part of who God wants her to be…a beautiful butterfly.

Reality Reflections

To walk through the process of change requires a certain amount of faith—a trust of being willing to step into the unknown. The questions may not have complete or rational answers. We think of Jesus' remarks to His disciples in Mark 10:14-15,

> *"Let the children come to me, and do not stop them, because the Kingdom of God belongs to such as these. I assure you that whoever does not receive the Kingdom of God like a child will never enter it."*

At times, change requires the faith and trust of an innocent child. We choose not to bargain or make deals with God. And, we wonder, how do we retrieve the faith that God blessed us with as children? So many changes in our lives, some we chose and others chosen for us, have piled so much hurt and pain on the child inside of us. It takes a tremendous amount of courage to take the risk to move all of it aside and dig deeper and deeper until at last we find what we need. This faith allows us to step out of our comfort zone and trust God. Because we have no answers to the myriad questions that will be tossed our direction by those who may not understand our choice, it will appear to be a lonely road. If we choose to follow the leading of the Spirit, we are assured that He will never leave us nor forsake us and that we are never alone.

The events surrounding the resurrection of Jesus called for change. In Luke 24:1-12 we read that on a Sunday morning, several women went to the tomb where Jesus' body had been placed. Their plans changed because the stone was no longer covering the opening. Instead of finding His body, they discovered an empty tomb and angels telling them not to be afraid. Jesus was not there; He was alive. They shared this change with the disciples, who thought they were crazy. Peter had to see for himself. He found the grave clothes and nothing else in the tomb.

Initially, the changes that are brought into our lives may seem crazy to us and to others. The nonsense of the situation may be that it was sudden and unexpected, just as it was when Jesus was no longer in the tomb. Change is often difficult to accept because it does not fit into the normal pattern of life.

When Peter entered the tomb he found the old clothes, which Jesus had discarded. Our old clothes bring a sense of comfortableness and sameness, but God is asking us to put on new clothes. He asks that we leave behind the old clothes of brokenness and put on the clothes of forgiveness and hope. We are asked to remove the clothes of fear and put on clothes of freedom and a new life. He encourages us to change into the "scrubs" of life and take God with us into the messy situations. Change is risky, but it also offers a new life. Is it worth the risk?

We know it is! Despite the constant change going on in our lives, especially in the last few months in the cocoon of C.P.E., God has assured us that we are following His call in our lives. Our wings have been pounding relentlessly through our spiritual metamorphosis and we are almost ready to break out of the chrysalis. Our enthusiasm and excitement is growing as we wait to see our beautiful new identities. Someday, when we've grown into our new wings, they will allow us to soar into a new life of love and freedom. Change has indeed become a beautiful reality in our lives. Without it, we would wither up and die, not having known the miracles that were just around the corner and the wholeness of being who God intends for us to be.

Fuel for your journey

1. Which story caused you to think of your own experiences? Why?

2. How does it make you feel?

3. What would you like to say to God right now?

4. Who can you share these feelings with?

CHAPTER FIVE

Identity
Removing the Masks

What picture comes to your mind when you hear the word *mask*? Is it a masquerade party, doctor or a nurse, a catcher's mask, Halloween trick-or-treating, a bank robber? Wearing a mask serves two purposes: protection, or concealing our identity. Some masks can make us laugh and feel good, while others are scary and cause fear. Masks can be healthy as we interchange them in response to our various roles in life. These are the masks that can't be seen. A person can wear all the masks of parent, spouse, sibling, child, worker, and friend at the same time.

Unhealthy masks are worn to conceal our identity. They also cover up feelings of fear, inadequacy and shame. We wear these masks so others will not see who we really are. Some masks we are forced to wear, to be what others expect us to be. Meeting the expectations of others is a difficult task. So to protect ourselves we accept the mask forced upon us.

It is possible to remove the masks one at a time and examine them carefully. As we look at them we can choose which are healthy masks and will allow our identity to shine through and be light and comfortable. The unhealthy masks cloud our vision and feel heavy and dark. These are the ones we need to discard. As the masks are taken off, our true identity is being revealed, the one that God had planned for us.

The combination of the identity that we are born with and the healthy masks, which we choose to keep, make us whole. We become a person that is confident in who we are. This freedom allows us to create loving relationships with others, ourselves and with God.

Lori

My Little Girl

We have learned through C.P.E. that our personality traits are formed by the age of two or three years old. Some studies have shown that these traits will remain the same the rest of our lives with very little change. This has taken me a long time to understand, because I feel that anyone can make a major change in his or her life if they have the will to do so and especially if they choose to follow a spiritual path. What I am realizing is that if I wish to find the personality that I was born with, before all of these things happened to me, I have to start to remove some of the masks I have learned to wear. There are times in my life when I long to be that small innocent child again. The three-year-old that knew God was calling her name when the priest said "Glory, Glory" during mass. But, the turmoil and challenges of life attempt to keep me from hearing God's voice that clearly. The weight of the masks muffle His voice and they hold me down like anchors tied to my spirit. The masks also become ugly over time as more and more are added. Imagine a beautiful piece of furniture that has been painted over and over again. Eventually, the paint begins to lift and crack. Now, imagine what happens when those layers of paint are slowly removed. The original, pure wood comes shining through, much like our original identity is revealed when all of the pain, disappointments, disapproval of others, criticisms and expectations are peeled away. Just like removing layers of paint, this transition takes time, energy, pain and strength.

As I'm recovering from the abuse, I'm learning how important it is to take care of my inner child. In the beginning I wondered how it was possible to take care of a little girl that was taken away from me so long ago. Now that I'm an adult it almost sounds silly that this child is still inside of me. But she is. The challenge for me is how to put aside all of the things that have kept me from being a child for so long and let her come out to play. In other words, how do I take off all of the masks I wear and get to who I really am? This is really hard work, but it is definitely worth it. Because my little girl was hurt so badly, my healing begins with her. As she heals I'm finding that I'm having more fun, doing silly things and laughing, really laughing.

Before I've been able to have this kind of fun, however, I've had to endure so much pain that at times I've felt devoured by it. This is the pain that I feel when another memory comes to the surface. Through this process of remembering, God blesses me with someone I love to comfort me and a wonderful feeling of peace when it's over. This is what keeps me going. This is the way that God encourages me to take the next step. Removing the mask of denial is slow and excruciating, but it's needed in order for the wounds below it to heal.

Hot Tears

About a year into my recovery, the flashbacks were increasing in intensity and details. Thanksgiving had passed very quietly. I welcomed the calmness of celebrating the day with Duane's family. I was going through a period of being immersed in the memories of abuse. It seemed as though I couldn't think of anything else. A few days after the holiday, I began to put up some Christmas decorations. Going through the boxes of treasures that we've collected over the years lifted my spirits a little. Christmas has always been my favorite holiday. It's a peaceful, sacred time for me now, but when I was little it was full of family fights, drinking and anger. I love to lie on the floor under the Christmas tree much like I did as a child. Looking up at the lights twinkling and smelling the pine needles seems very magical to me. I remember getting lost in the magic when I was little, as the turmoil went on around me. I would ask Santa Claus to come get me and take me to where there was no fighting, just love.

The Christmas that I was five, I received a Santa Claus toy. It was a stuffed doll, with a bright red suit, a cheery face and a long white beard. On the back was a key, which wound up the music box inside, and it played Christmas songs. I loved it. I took it everywhere with me and slept with it at night. When the holiday was over and the decorations were put away, Mom said that the Santa needed to be packed away for next Christmas. It was hard to let go of him, but I did as I was told. I could hardly wait until the year was over and I could hold him again for a couple of weeks. As I got older, Santa was unpacked and became part of the decorations. I secretly looked forward to seeing him every year even though I had grown up. The Christmas after Duane and I were married, my Santa Claus came home with me. I still have him. He's forty years old, his suit is tattered and faded, the music box will not play and his beard is now gray, but I still bring him out every year. He has become a part of me.

So as I was decorating the house this last Christmas, I found my Santa Claus in a box. I took him out and held him as I did as a child. During this time of being overwhelmed with all the memories of abuse, I felt very comforted by holding the doll. At night I placed him on my nightstand and would hold him if I felt afraid or if I had a nightmare. He made me feel safe again.

A few days before Christmas, I had gone to bed early but couldn't sleep. I was feeling very anxious and afraid. When Duane came to bed, he found me curled up on my side, holding the doll. Then I felt the shaking begin. I lay there clinging to the beard of my Santa, and Duane sat next to me trying to comfort me through the flashback. The memories were very strong and frightening. I began answering Duane in my little girl voice as he asked me questions. I told him that my daddy had a tattoo and I traced it on his arm with my finger to show him where it was. I started to cry and Duane told me over and over that I was safe, that I was with him. I cried harder and began to rock, still clinging to Santa's beard. Then Duane took my hand and placed it on his face, on his beard. He told me, "It's me, you're safe, see……feel my beard, it's me." In that moment the little girl inside of me met Duane. I patted his beard with one hand and held Santa's with the other. As I began to calm down, my tears became very hot. I cried and kept patting Duane's beard. My little girl realized that a man with a beard had finally come and had taken her away from the fights and had given her love. Those tears had been inside of me for more than forty years, stuffed way down, waiting for the man with a beard. My eyes and cheeks burned as the tears rolled down my face. I lay there for a long time holding onto Santa and Duane. My past had become my present. They were one in the same. All the layers of pain that had hidden my little girl's tears were stripped away in a magical moment. I had found her and she has her identity back because of this man with a beard.

After the flashback had ended and I was calm again, Duane and I went to the living room, spread blankets on the floor and lay together under the Christmas tree. It was so beautiful. I realized that God had heard the prayers of a little girl long ago. The Santa Claus was a promise of what was to come. Not only did He bring Duane into my life as the man with the beard, but He brought Urias also. He, too, has a wonderful beard that is as white as my Santa's was forty years ago. I have been so blessed by

God and I am forever grateful. So I now I have three men with beards, Duane, Urias and Santa. After Christmas was over this year, my Santa has found a special place in the house where I can look at him all the time. I will never pack him away again. Because for me, with God's love, every day can be Christmas with its peace, sacredness and magical moments. All I have to do is hold my Santa and remember my little girl's hot tears.

Sis

Since my first brother was born when I was two years old, I have had the identity of the oldest child. If you have ever heard of the birth order studies that have been done, you are probably aware of the traits that are common with firstborn people. We are very responsible, dependable, serious and courageous. These characteristics and the strength and determination I gained from the abuse have all been mixed together and have formed my identity as a sister. I have been very proud of this identity for as long as I can remember. As soon as my brothers and sister were born I wanted to help take care of them. I have been there for every part of their lives. They have not known life without me. We have been through so much together. We have experienced the same joys and the same sadness. Every time the arguments started between Mom and Dad, we stuck together and comforted each other.

As we got older and I was given the responsibility of watching the other kids, the fighting between us began. My oldest brother and I were the ones that fought the hardest. As I look back, I realize that he must have felt that I was his boss and I was only two years older. Some of the fights we had were very intense and violent. I regret that our relationship continued in this way through most of our teen years. But, I know that we were reacting to the stress within the home and we didn't know any other ways of coping. Fortunately, after I married and left home, we began getting along better.

My identity as a sister is one of the masks that I needed to remove in order to discover who I truly am. By always being there for the others and ignoring my own feelings and needs, I lost sight of my own personality. It became buried under the masks. The problems within the family in the last few years have been painful, but essential for me to move beyond everyone else's issues and focus on my own. Removing this mask continues to be a difficult work in progress. I have learned that there is a big part of me that thrives on taking care of others. This trait is part of my identity as a sister who has grown up in a dysfunctional home. It's what I feel comfortable doing. This is who I am. Being a caretaker has played a part in my decision to become a chaplain. But, before I could provide care to patients and families, I needed to take the time to care for myself. Otherwise, my issues would get in the way of being totally present with others. My passion for helping people has fueled my commitment to completely knowing myself and using my past hurts to connect on a very deep level with those that are in pain.

In the process of taking care of myself, my identity as a sister has been put aside. I'm praying that it is only temporary, but with the feelings that my family has for me, it's very difficult to hang on to that identity. I have wondered for a long time if for some reason one of my siblings needed me, if I would be there for them, even though they have not been there for me. The adult part of me would like to walk away and leave them to take care of themselves. But, my little girl is urging me to be the big sister, no matter what. She doesn't hold grudges or wish for revenge. When I look back on my recovery, I can see that there have been times when the exact opposite was what I wanted to do. I wanted them to hurt, too. Those feelings have overwhelmed me during periods of deep pain and rejection. So I continue to wonder, what I will do when faced with the situation.

One evening recently, I was driving home from work. The weather had been stormy all day long, with the threat of tornadoes across the state. It began raining very hard and I turned the radio up a little so I could hear it. The announcer came on with a bulletin that a tornado had been spotted in the county where some of my family lives. I felt like my heart stopped when I heard that it was very near their homes. I turned the volume up higher and suddenly looked up. The traffic light at the intersection ahead of me had turned red. I quickly hit my brakes and was able to stop in time. My reaction to the possible danger for my family startled me. And, at the same time, I was happy that I reacted as I did. Later, I thanked God that there had been no injuries or damage from the tornado. I also thanked Him for helping me to answer my question. I am very certain that if any of my family ever needs me that I will be there for them. Even if my presence isn't accepted, I will help them the best way I know of, which is to pray.

"I Just Want To Be Me"

As I have gone through the process of removing my masks and deciding which ones are distorting my view and holding me back, I have made many significant discoveries about my various identities. Some have been easier to let go of than others. And, there are those that have become such a part of who I am, that it has been difficult to separate where I leave off and someone else begins.

For as long as I can remember I have always struggled to be a separate identity from my mom. Long before I realized that the abuse in our home was not a "normal" thing, I had vowed to never treat my children in the same way. The freedom that I always dreamed of and never really had has formed a mask of determination, which I will continue to wear. But, for many years, this mask had been hidden from me. It took a lot of hard work to find it and it takes more work to keep the determination healthy and not let in turn into stubbornness or rigidity. These are some of the traits of the mask that my mom wears.

When Jase and Krystina were about twelve and seven, Margaret asked me how I was able to discipline the kids without treating them the way my parents had treated me. I thought about that for a long time and came to realize that first of all Duane was teaching me how to be a parent, but also that every time I needed to give a punishment, my first thought was how would my mom react to this situation and then I did the opposite of what she would do. This meant that the kids were sent to their rooms instead of hit with a belt, privileges were taken away and favorite toys were put up for a while. But, one thing that I did not want to take from them was their freedom. So, I've learned to pick my battles. As they grow older, I am growing with them. We have learned a lot together. I do have regrets for some of the things I did, or didn't do and should have, but I am grateful that each of the kids are comfortable sharing their opinions and feelings with us and they have never been physically or emotionally hurt. Duane and I are very proud of the adults that our children have grown into.

As I said, my struggle to not be my mom has lasted many, many years. Even when I knew that I was not reacting in ways that she would, I still worried that somehow it would happen if I let my guard down. She once told me that she hoped that I would someday have a son or daughter that would treat me in the same way that I've treated her. Those words have haunted me for all of my adult life, which fed my worry that I would become like my mother, and my relationship with my kids would be the same. That has not happened, but it was only a few months ago that I finally let go of her words.

Around Christmas time, Jason gave us the news that we had been dreading since he was born. He wanted to move to Florida and finish school there. Jase has grown into a wonderful, funny, loving man and I enjoy being around him. Our relationship has been changing from that of parent/child to an adult level of respect for one another. In some ways, I've known that he would want to go off on his own someday since he has always been independent and adventurous. My greatest prayer for both of my kids is that they are happy, wherever they are, and my goal is to support them in their dreams. So even though I knew I would miss him a great deal, I also knew that I had to let him go. Duane and I began making plans to help him move, while our hearts were beginning to make the adjustment of not being near him.

The months went by quickly and by March, Jason had found an apartment in Naples, Florida. The date was set, the rental truck was reserved and he began packing. All of sudden this seemed too real. Every time I looked at him I wanted to hold him and cry. I tried my best to be strong. Duane and I reminded each other that he would only be a few hours away by plane and we would plan to visit him often. Jason was so excited to go and his excitement was contagious. But, underneath the fun and laughter the tears hovered close to the surface.

Then the night before the move was upon us. Everything was packed and ready to go. We were planning to leave early the next morning. As we were making final preparations, Jason came home. He walked through the kitchen door and fell into Duane's arms. Reality had set in and he was having second thoughts. The three of us stood wrapped in each other's arms and cried. Jase was saying that he couldn't leave his best friend, his dad. In that moment it would have been so incredibly easy to persuade him to stay near us. I wanted to say the words, "Then, don't go," but instead I heard myself saying, "But, Jase, this is your dream." We assured him that no matter where he went, he would never leave us, that we would always be together. Eventually, our tears subsided and he was sure that he was making the right decision to go. By this time, we were all exhausted so we went to bed. But Duane and I didn't sleep. We just held each other and cried most of the night.

We have survived this change in our lives. Jason is settled in his apartment and has found a wonderful job. In the midst of my grief, however, I found a blessing. Sara and I talked about what had happened the night before Jase left home. When I told her what I had said to him, she grabbed my hand and asked me, "Do you know what this means?" I didn't, so she told me, "You are not your mom. You were able to let him go. Your mother couldn't do that for you, but you did it for Jase." Finally, the ghost of my mom's words has left me. I no longer worry about her identity sneaking up on me. My identity as mom to Jason and Krystina is healthy and alive. This is a mask that I am very proud to wear for all to see.

"So Who Am I?"

As I've reflected on my identities and what God has asked me to do, I've come to the realization of how all the things I have gone through have created the person I am today. In the midst of the pain of my childhood, I somehow found the strength to survive. By facing my past I have tapped into a great well of compassion for others in pain. As I've removed the mask of letting the family control me, these identities of strength and compassion have been exposed and I am learning to look at myself in a new way. Each time I look in the mirror it becomes a little easier to see me instead of the strong resemblance to my father. Sr. Anne's words still comfort me when the image looking back at me is cloudy and out of focus.

Building my identity feels like putting together a jigsaw puzzle. Before I met Duane, my life's puzzle was incomplete, with gaping holes where pieces were missing or lost. Even my straight edges were crooked, broken and going in different directions. Over the years I found several pieces that I knew were important to the whole picture, but there was no guide or example for me to follow, so these pieces were put aside.

My relationship with Margaret helped me to straighten my edges and place them in a row that would eventually connect me with God's love. When this happened, God helped me to see that the inside of my puzzle was chaos. With my boundaries firmly in place, I began looking at each puzzle piece to identify where it belonged or if it should be in a completely different one altogether. These pieces symbolized my low self-esteem, fear and shame. Once I had removed them, the parts of myself that were necessary to the puzzle became clear and I found where they fit perfectly. My strength interlocked with my confidence. Compassion and love became inseparable. Joy, peace and fun connected with the little girl inside of me to form a beautiful butterfly within this puzzle of my life.

Because of God's promises to me, my puzzle is expanding and growing into an unbelievable landscape, in which the butterfly within me travels through my past, my present and my future. Wherever she flies, the pieces seem to fall into place. The view is breathtaking and she can see the areas when God had asked her to surrender an identity she loved. It was difficult, but she obeyed. Now she is seeing that what she thought was a surrender was actually putting the piece aside for the moment in order to focus on another identity. Eventually, God will bring it back into the picture and it will fit in a completely different way than it had before.

This is a portrait of me, complete with all of my healthy identities. This is also a work in progress, because I'm still changing. But, who I am right now is someone that I really like. The sum of my identities shows that I am a child of God, a wife, a mom, a friend, a sister, a child, a woman, a person and a chaplain. Removing the masks has revealed the innocence of my faith in God. Just as I heard my name being called in church when I was little, I now hear God calling me by the name He had given me so long ago, Glori. This is my new name. God has taken the good in my life and combined it with the name my parents gave me to form one identity in His eyes. Without the heaviness of the masks I once wore, my vision and hearing are clear. The barriers are gone. My faith allows me to hear Him calling, "Glori, Glori," loud and clear. The final piece of my life's puzzle will fall into place when I finally stand before Him, face to face, and hear Him say, "Welcome home, my Glori."

Sara

Search for Identity

I made an interesting discovery as I consulted the dictionary for the meaning of identity. I learned it means either individuality or the condition of being the same as a person or group. This appeared to be a strange dichotomy. How could I experience the sameness within a group and also retain my individuality? Does sameness destroy my individuality? These are questions that I struggled with as I considered my identity.

My mother tells me that as a young child I would sing and dance and strut around as if I owned the world. What happened to this confident, free child in my past? I believe she felt pressured to conform. I valued sameness above my individuality. There are stages in our life as we develop our identity when conformity is most important.

As an adolescent I had a slumber party in our meadow along the creek. We were busy chatting about girl issues, and I remember expressing that I wished I could wear a necklace. Wearing of jewelry was not permitted in the Mennonite Church as I was growing up. It was necessary that I conform and not cause my parents or myself any problems. My identity was encompassed with the need to conform to the rules of the Mennonite Church. It was only after I left home as a young adult that I wore my first necklace. It was a gold cross, given to me by some close friends. I'm sure they had no idea that I had never worn a necklace until they gave me their gift.

Adolescence is a time of struggle when most people search for their identity. Many people compared me to my mother as I was growing up. Mother had a round face and I would stand in front of the mirror and pull my face down trying to make it appear longer. When I went to Bible school in Canada, it was to an area where nobody knew my parents. This was the first time I attempted to develop my own identity. In this environment I learned to play cards, party a little, wear slacks, and not wear a prayer veil to church. The sparks flew when I returned home and I felt misunderstood when I wore slacks without wearing them underneath a skirt. Finding my own identity was painful and it brought conflict. Since one of my "laws" was to please my parents I found it difficult to go against their wishes. But I stood my ground and continued to wear slacks without a skirt. Today, my mother also wears slacks.

In society our vocation gives us a sense of identity. For twenty years in certain settings I identified myself as a licensed practical nurse. Sometimes I was the mother of Heidi and Heather or the wife of Les. When I began the C.P.E. program I identified myself as Chaplain Sara. Does our profession give us a sense of identity? When we become a stay-at-home mom or retire, how do we identify ourselves? Who are we under the mask of our occupation?

Our name is important to us. When I was a child I was called by my full name, Sara Ann. This continued until I was in third grade. My teacher dropped my middle name and I was Sara. That year was a time of transition as I moved from a one-room setting to the larger elementary school. I changed schools and my name was changed. My identity was altered against my wishes. Several years later I was called Sis by my siblings, and outside the home I was known as Sara. I wished my parents had given me a more common name. I would have chosen the name Sharon. As an adult, I appreciate my given name because it means "princess." I look upon myself as being chosen by God to be part of His royal family. I have a new identity in God's family.

Today we hear much of people's identity being stolen. We are told to shred our important papers because others may use the numbers that identify who we are to the business, government and medical world. This has become a disturbing situation; I witnessed the trauma a friend went through when her wallet was stolen. She felt that she had been violated. Our personal matters become known to a stranger.

A situation like this can be devastating, but it is sadder when a person has their personhood snatched from them. In order to right the wrong that had been committed against my friend she found it necessary to make numerous phone calls. The same holds true when our personhood is distorted or robbed by others. We feel violated and want to hide from others; instead, we will grow stronger if we face the situation and remain true to ourselves and who we are.

For almost six months I had the privilege to give pastoral care to a cancer support group. This was part of my training in the C.P.E. program. As I opened myself to them, they in turn gave me the gift of relationship. Each person had either heard the diagnosis of cancer given to him or her or to his or her loved one. The word *cancer* changed their identity from that moment. As I listened to their stories I understood that they had the choice to view themselves as victims or as survivors. With the support of each other they were able to become survivors. This is a group of strong people who have grown, because they did not allow cancer to destroy their identity, but rather give their identity a broader dimension.

As a child, I was exposed to multicultural situations, and my experience expanded as a young adult. Since we moved to Michigan, some of my closest friends have been from another culture. My friends from India, Pakistan and the Philippines adopted me into their families as a "grandma" for their children. I discovered this interaction to be fun and stimulating. During my third unit of C.P.E. I had a classmate accuse me of not being sensitive to racial issues. This accusation felt like a direct blow to my personhood. My integrity was being questioned and also the values by which I lived.

As a chaplain in the hospital I frequently provided care to African-American and Hispanic families. A white woman walking into a room filled with others of a different skin color causes an obvious distinction. As I build a relationship with the family members, my identity moves from that of an individual to that of sameness. In the heart, emotions and soul, there is common ground. We connect on a spiritual level and know comfort and camaraderie. I will always be a white woman, but my soul has become multicultural. I'm content and comfortable with this identity.

Removal of the Masks

Attending the Racial Ethnic Multicultural conference, in February 2004, was a powerful and empowering experience for me. REM is an arm of the Association for Clinical Pastoral Education. Lori and I, as Caucasians, were in the minority, but were received with open arms and love. It was as I gathered with my sisters and brothers that I was able to return to the spontaneity and freedom of my inner child. The first evening as we stood worshiping and praising the Lord, I felt as free as a little girl sitting on Grandpa's lap, enjoying being present with him. I tend to be very intense, focused and goal-orientated. That evening I released my inner child. I had been praying for several weeks that God's Spirit would minister to Lori and myself in a special way. I began to feel God's healing touch on my spirit. The last session, I was anointed with oil by a sister of color and the Holy Spirit filled me. I found a new freedom in my identity. The mask of pleasing others was allowed to fall to the ground and new life has burst forth. I will never be the same and it has been awesome that my new life came forth in a multicultural setting.

Another mask that fell to the ground was that of being serious and intense in my relationship with God. While in Chicago for the REM Conference, we went out on Friday night to enjoy the city of Chicago. Whit, a fellow resident, had the honor of being our tour guide. It was a memorable experience as we were on the ninety-sixth floor of the Hancock building when several firemen walked out of the elevator. They began exploring an area in the ceiling where the attendants had smelled smoke. Fortunately it was a false alarm. We were wild with excitement as we had our picture taken with the firemen. We had an evening of laughter and fun: eating pizza, drinking coffee at Starbucks late at night, finding our way around the city, and visiting the lobby of an exclusive hotel. We did not get back to our hotel until after midnight and we were exhausted. I had thrown the mask of responsibility away for the evening.

I made an awesome discovery the next morning. God did not require that I spend time in fasting and prayer for Him to hear the cry of my heart. He knew my heart's desire for deeper fellowship. I could have fun on the town the night before and God still answered my longings. God laughs and enjoys seeing us have fun and then as any loving person would do, gives us even more to celebrate.

Why did I connect so deeply with these African American women? In reading their theology and stories, I'm learning the value of openness of reality to life experiences. This is where we found common ground. My German heritage is non-expressive and stoic. Life is real and understood only as it can be explained. The spirit within me longed for a freedom of expression. Even as a child I found comfort in God being present with me. It was much like sitting on Grandpa's lap, feeling special and chosen. We never talked much but we just sat and enjoyed the presence of each other. This is what I often find myself doing with God, cuddling up underneath His wings, knowing the warmth and protection that is available to me. I find the cleft in the rock that protects me from the storms of life. God provides for me the security and strength that I need.

Holy Spirit at Work

As a young adult, the Holy Spirit's work in me became very important. The Spirit could not be explained, but I felt and experienced the results of His work. When my marriage was "on the rocks" it was to the Spirit I turned for comfort and direction. The scripture of Isaiah 58:11-12 became very meaningful to me;

"The Lord will guide you always; he will satisfy your needs in a sun-scorched land and will strengthen your frame. You will be like a well-watered garden, like a spring whose waters never fail. Your people will rebuild the ancient ruins and will raise up the age-old foundations; you will be called Repairer of Broken Walls, Restorer of Streets with Dwellings."

I identified with the writer that I was living in a sun-scorched land. But, I believed by faith that some day I would become a well-watered garden. As the years went by I began to believe that God was training and empowering me to not only repair my life, but also help others find the hope and courage they need to repair and restore their life situations.

At REM as I was free to once again open myself up to the work of the Holy Spirit. I experienced a freedom and a new identity; a calling to share with others the possibility of healing and wholeness. God had provided for me a place of safety where I would receive care and nurturing as He spoke to my heart. There was a burning and renewing within that I could not explain, it was mystical and needed no explanation. Those who were able to connect with my soul understood and affirmed me. God is calling me to a new identity through the refining fire of His Spirit. The identities of the past are being burned and in their place is springing forth a new life.

Selfhood Reflections

Who am I? Why was I born? Does my life have a purpose? When we are in the midst of struggles and difficulties, these are questions that come to our mind. The writer of Psalm 139:13-16, tells us that God knows our identity from beginning to end. God knit us together in our mother's womb. God was aware of us even before we were born. Before we took our first breath

God planned each day of our life. The prophet Jeremiah also tells us that God has plans for each of us. Plans to prosper us and not to bring us harm. Plans to give us hope and a future. The closer our relationship is to God the more easily we can know and understand the direction we should travel in the journey of life.

In the Old Testament, Genesis 32, we find Jacob, a man with many troubles. He talked his brother, Esau into selling his birthright for a pot of stew. In order to escape the wrath of an angry brother, he traveled to his Uncle Laban's home. While there he fell in love with Rachel and volunteered to work seven years for his uncle if he could marry Rachel. When the seven years were complete Jacob was tricked into marrying Rachel's sister, Leah. So he worked seven more years to earn the right to marry Rachel.

Jacob's love for Rachel was all consuming. The desire to marry her became his main focus and he was willing to do whatever was necessary. We have found that becoming a chaplain has given us something in common with Jacob. We, too have a passion that has become all consuming. Our commitment to C.P.E. required us to make this goal our main priority. God surprised us in the process and asked us to change our focus once again. We had no intention of writing a book when we entered C.P.E., but God had different plans. C.P.E. has given us the ability to become willing to look at our masks in order for us to share ourselves with others.

Finally, it was time for Jacob to return home, which meant meeting his brother, Esau. It was the night before this meeting that Jacob wrestled with God. It was through this experience Jacob's identity was changed. Jacob was alone and wrestled with a man all night. The man said it was time for him to go, but Jacob asked that he bless him before he left. The man replied that his name would be changed to Israel, which means, "He struggles with God," and the man blessed Jacob. The place of this interaction Jacob called Peniel meaning "the face of God."

After this experience, Jacob had acquired a limp as a result of the wrestling.

In reflecting upon our times of identity change, we feel a connection with Jacob. Our struggles with identity take place when we are alone. It is then that we wrestle with God. We come face to face with our own limitations and God's ultimate plans for us. We mark verses in our Bible or record in our journaling moments of decision and renewal so they are remembered. These are "Peniel moments" for us, when we came face to face with God. We try to see these moments of struggles as blessings from God as He is changing us from one identity to another. Until, at last, we have found our true self, the identity we were born with and we fully believe that we are children of God.

Fuel for your journey

1. Which story caused you to think of your own experiences? Why?

2. How does it make you feel?

3. What would you like to say to God right now?

4. Who can you share these feelings with?

CHAPTER SIX

Honoring our Bodies

Made in God's Image

What does it mean to honor our bodies? What does God intend it to mean? It seems that we have been struggling with these questions since time began. With the advances that have been made in society throughout the centuries, the beauty of our bodies have become distorted and twisted into something far from God's intentions. We have become more concerned with what others think of us than with the beautiful body that God created for each of us before we were born.

There are many reasons that we have become uncomfortable with our bodies. Low self-esteem, sexual and verbal abuse are just a few of the causes of women's, especially young girls', obsessions with how their bodies look. What they see in the mirror is what others see, not what God sees. During one hour of watching TV recently, there were two commercials to lose weight, three ads for makeup and hair color, one showing the results of plastic surgery and another for equipment to get the "perfect abs." With all of this pressure to conform to society's image, how do we stay true to ourselves?

We can begin by recognizing how we honor other things in our lives, such as our children, our homes, our careers, etc. Then take our bodies and include them in this list. Look around and find the most precious gift someone has given you. Hold it, admire it, keep it safe and love it. Now, imagine your body as this precious gift, hold it, admire it, keep it safe and love it. This is how God wants us to honor our bodies. You are a special gift from God and His image of you is beautiful and treasured and honored, forever.

Sara
Learning Body Care

Heidi has begun a business of helping women care for their skin and teaching them to apply makeup to produce an attractive appearance. I spent an afternoon having her do a makeover for me. Heidi taught me how to apply eye cosmetics so my eyes became more noticeable. A little bit of blush applied at the proper place brightened my face. When she was finished I had a natural glow about me.

When Heidi had spoken with me about the possibility of becoming involved with a cosmetic business, she was guarded, wondering about my reaction. During the last year I have become impressed with how important it is for people to care for their bodies and make them as attractive as possible. My reply to her was that helping women to feel good about themselves is an important ministry. She could have fun applying makeup, help others, and also provide some additional income.

Traditionally, I was taught that makeup was sinful, and feeling any pride about self was giving place to the devil. The body form was to be concealed and no attention should be drawn to it. At Bible school, I remember a young man mentioning to several girls that we should be aware of how we dress. I believe there is a difference between being seductive and being attractive. When our appearance is attractive others are drawn to us.

As females we have been created in God's image and the Creator declared the creation very good. God was pleased with the female form given to our body. By honoring our body we agree with the Creator's evaluation. What does it mean to honor our body? When we honor our body we respect, like, esteem, regard and give deference to our physical form. We listen to our body and become its friend.

When I push myself too much my body pays the price. I turn a deaf ear to its message until the pain becomes too great and finally my body gets the attention of my brain. There have been situations when my neck was hurting because I did an activity that was not wise. I pretend that I'm not experiencing any pain and maybe if I don't think about the pain, it will disappear. Never does that happen, because my body is trying to give me a message that I need to lie down and give my neck some relaxation.

Our body needs the proper nourishment, sleep and exercise if it is to function as God intended. Often we tend to put the needs of others before our own, and our body becomes exhausted and deteriorates. We get dark circles under our eyes, we gain or lose excessive weight, or become so tired we cannot sleep at night. These are signals that we should slow down and take time to develop a relationship with our body.

Moments of Enlightenment

Because we are mortals there will be times when disease or deterioration invades our body. I remember an experience on the Surgical Intensive Care Unit. A woman had struggled several days with complications following open-heart surgery.

I entered the room and looked at the form lying in the bed. She looked more like a bloated monster than a human being. The odor was nauseating. The family stood in the room staring out the window, unable to be close to their mother. I was overcome with the ugliness and deformity of the body. I was angry at what medical science has attempted to accomplish but instead had disfigured this woman. The patient was unresponsive and the family was aware she would soon die.

As happens so often, the Holy Spirit gave me direction for this heart-wrenching situation. I walked to her bedside and took her huge, swollen hand between my hands. I spoke her name and reminded her that her family was present and that they loved her. I stroked her forehead and she died.

This woman was no longer able to honor her body, but in touching her I gave her honor. Regardless of the appearance of the body it needs to be honored. We don't look at the disease or disfigurement. We see beyond that to the soul of the person.

When I returned to the classroom I was visibly shaken. I was angry and felt like throwing up. Urias asked me to reflect upon my experience theologically. I was not able to, so he helped me. He explained that how I felt seeing and smelling this woman is how God feels when He looks at our sin. As God reached out to us by sending Jesus to die for our sin so He could look at us, I did the same thing by reaching out and touching this woman. Just as Jesus gives us honor before God, I was able to give the patient honor before she died.

Healthy Body Concepts

There is a difference between honoring our body and worshiping our body. When our body becomes a fixation and the main focus of our life, we have allowed our body to become our god. If on the other hand, we respect and tend to our body, it is an act of worship to God, because we are giving honor to the Creator.

It has been difficult for me over the years to give honor to my body. I felt that the body was of less importance than the spirit. In some ways the body was evil. The feelings that the body produced within me were disturbing and to be stuffed into the darkest corners. God had given me a female body that was created to bring my husband and myself pleasure, but I was afraid to acknowledge those feelings. I could not experience orgasm because I was afraid to allow my body to feel the pleasure that came with sexual intercourse. As I began to accept myself as a woman and rejoice in the fact that I was created a woman, I opened myself to the blessings God gave to me because I am a woman.

When I was unpacking my books after a recent move, I was reminiscing and remembering when I read or studied the books on my shelf. I leafed through a book I had studied a number of years ago in a small group setting. There was a reflective section speaking of our relationship to God as two tuning forks of the same kind—both of them vibrate when one of them is struck. I had underlined many important thoughts in that chapter, but noticed an unnoted paragraph likening the Spirit to a skillful lover who knows exactly how to turn us on. At that time I could not identify with that statement because I was afraid to allow myself to have feelings that a skillful lover could bring to me.

As I have learned to honor my body, my husband also treats my body with more respect and gentleness. No longer is my body only to meet his physical needs. We have found pleasure and compatibility in each other, as God had planned at the time of creation.

God created female and male each in a different way. Our bodies appear different and have different hormones flowing through them. Females are of no lesser value than males, just different. We can find harmony rather than discord in our differences. In an orchestra each instrument looks different, but as they blend together, playing different notes the result is beautiful music.

Lori

A New Confidence

I have learned that in order for me to honor my body, I first had to understand why I am the way I am. My image of my body has always been distorted by the sexual abuse I received as a child. Until the memories returned, I could never understand why I've always worn clothes big enough to hide my shape. I have never worn a bathing suit without a T-shirt over it. There were hot summers that I refused to wear shorts because my legs would show. So many times I became angry at Duane if he would walk into our bedroom and find me undressed. I didn't understand the anger and the shame I felt at my body. Now I know the reasons behind my feelings, and realizing that these are normal reactions to someone who has been abused has given me the freedom to direct the anger where it belongs and not at Duane or myself. This knowledge has also given me permission to be comfortable with my body, to wear shorts and a bathing suit and especially to be who I am without worrying about other's opinions of me.

Just a few weeks ago, I was getting ready to go to a graduation party and I put on a new skirt that I had just bought. It was a plain, khaki-colored skirt that was about four inches above my knee. Now, for twenty-six years Duane has tried to get me to wear a shorter skirt, but I always chose the long ones that covered my legs. But, when I was shopping, my newly found adventurous spirit gave me the courage to take a risk and try on a new style. When I did, I felt free and comfortable. I liked what I saw in the mirror. So I dressed for the party and when Duane came around the corner and saw me, he let out a very enthusiastic "whoo-eee." I just smiled and let the feeling of being attractive sink in. That was a powerful moment in my life.

My new confidence in myself has brought Duane and me even closer to each other than we've ever been. I'm not ashamed for him to see my body any longer. He has been incredibly patient with me as I've gone through this process of recovery. I don't know why he didn't give up on me a long time ago, but I'll be forever grateful to him for his unending love for me.

Gracie

Taking care of myself and honoring my body is new to me and I've taken many baby steps along the way. Shortly after I began seeing my therapist, she suggested that I might want to read the book, *The Courage to Heal*, written by Ellen Bass and Laura Davis, for adult survivors of childhood sexual abuse. This is a wonderful book and it has helped me tremendously. Reading about other survivors' experiences brought me comfort in knowing that I wasn't alone. The authors also give valuable advice on self-care while going through the process of healing. One of the exercises recommended is to make a list of ways that you can nurture yourself and find comfort in the midst of your pain.

I decided that this was a good idea for me, since I wasn't very good at taking care of myself. So one afternoon, I sat down to make a list of what would help me feel better. It wasn't long before I became very discouraged. After so many years of neglecting myself and taking care of others, I had no idea what I wanted that would be just for me. I struggled to come up with ideas like listening to music or going for walks. Nothing I thought of seemed right for me. I managed to put down three or four ideas and for some reason I wrote, "Get a new puppy." I looked at that entry and wondered why I even wrote it down. I closed my book and decided I had wasted my time.

Later that day, I was sitting with Duane on our swing in the backyard and I told him that I was upset at myself for not being able to come up with one thing on my list that was doable. He asked me what was on the list, so I went and brought back my book for him to see. We looked at each one and I had reasons why nothing would work. I didn't even mention the new puppy, I just crossed it off the list. He noticed and asked me why a dog wasn't possible. I gave him every reason I could think of; we already have one dog, Barney, our black lab, Maggie the cat, I worked too many hours at the hospital, we were getting new carpeting in a couple of weeks, the expense, the time, the mess and so on and so on. For every reason I gave, Duane had an answer for it. I finally said that it just wouldn't work right now, maybe in a few months or so. He took my hand and looked at me tenderly and said, "If a puppy is what it takes to help you feel better, then we'll get a puppy, now." All of a sudden my bad mood lifted and I heard myself answer him, "Okay, but it has to be a chocolate lab, a female and her name is Gracie." Then I realized that God had told me to write the idea on my list and that He already had her waiting somewhere for me. I just had to find her. And, so the search began.

We looked everywhere for this dog. I was going to be on vacation from work for a couple of weeks and so we wanted to find a pup that was ready to go in that time frame. This was not an easy task and once again I became discouraged. We had decided that we wanted a purebred lab with papers because I thought it would be a good idea to train her to be a therapy dog. Someday I'd be able to visit patients and families with her. But, the cost for a registered puppy was very expensive. Everywhere we called, the pups were either too young or too much money. I was ready to give up.

The first day of my vacation was also the day the new carpeting was being installed in our living room. There wasn't much I could do, except stay out of the worker's way, so I decided to call a few more places. I told myself that if I couldn't find a pup that day, it just wasn't meant to be. I looked through the phone book for breeders and found one that was only a few miles from our home, in fact we've driven past it many times over the years. I called and spoke to the owner, who told me that they had several chocolate lab puppies that were ready to go. A little bit of hope surfaced and then sank when he told me that the price for the pups was $500. All of the pets we've had have either been free or very little money, I just couldn't justify spending that much. I thanked the breeder for his time, but we couldn't afford it. I explained that we just wanted a family dog; we didn't plan to breed her or show her, but having papers was important for her therapy training. Then he told me about a ten-week-old chocolate female that he could sell for less because she had a flaw. My heart started to break for her and I asked him what was wrong with her. He said, "She's perfect, except she has an overbite." She wouldn't be able to be bred or shown because of it. I thought to myself that this pup and I would get along very well, since I have flaws too. I made arrangements to meet with the breeder later that afternoon.

When Duane and I arrived and met this little ball of brown fur, needless to say, we immediately fell in love with her. We began calling her Gracie right away; no other name would be right for her. She is perfect and her overbite hardly shows. The breeder sold her to us for about two hundred dollars less and we've decided that she is worth every penny. As Gracie was getting ready to come home with us (bath, nails, ears, the works), the owner told us her story. Her father's name is Job and her mother is Chloe. She was the only pup in the litter, which is extremely unusual. It seems that the part of Job that sits in the snow became frostbitten and when he thawed out, there was only enough to produce one pup, my Gracie. She has been special from the beginning. She was chosen just for me.

Even though Gracie is not officially a therapy dog as yet, she has been my therapy since the moment I first held her. She makes me laugh when I need to. She helps me to see the wonder of nature as she sees things for the first time. And, she loves me unconditionally. We are a lot alike, also. We both have brown hair and eyes and we share a love for popcorn. When she was six months old, she passed her obedience training with flying colors and won a blue ribbon. Our next step is to take the therapy dog training when she's a year old. Then I'll be able to share with others how God taught me to honor my body by nurturing it with love. Since Gracie has been in my life, my baby steps have turned into leaps of faith. My list of ways to nurture myself has grown longer and my body has benefited from it. At the top of the list will always be "spend time with Gracie" because she knows what I need. She's my gift of Grace from God. Her official name on the registered papers reads, "Alpha Omega's Lady of Grace." But, God knew her before she was born and He called her Gracie. His gift to me was there, I just had to look and have faith until I found it.

Boundaries

Another important way of honoring our bodies is to establish boundaries. These are rules that we have for ourselves to prevent others from taking advantage of us. In healthy, functional families, parents will help their children to develop their boundaries by being respectful of each other. But, when these conditions do not exist or there is no one to teach us, we grow up allowing people to hurt and abuse us. Growing up in an abusive situation, I learned by my parents' actions and examples that my body, mind and spirit did not deserve respect. With no boundaries in place to protect me, I've allowed the family and others to control my life and use me in whatever way they wanted.

In the last few years I've begun to recognize when someone's actions are not acceptable to me. The most difficult part for me is letting the person know when they've crossed the line. In some cases, those people have not respected my boundaries regardless of what I say, so I've removed myself from them. There are others that I am always on guard with, because even though I've explained my situation very clearly, they sometimes try to find a way around it.

One of my boundary issues is with inappropriate touch. I understand now that this is a result of the abuse, and at the age of forty-five, I need to create the rules to live my life by. I have always been very sensitive to anyone touching me, especially if I don't see it coming. There are several relatives in the family that love to poke me in my side or grab me from behind. Even though I became angry, I rarely said anything to them. I let the abuse continue. Confrontation is not something that I'm good at and I haven't felt comfortable standing up for myself. God knows this, so He arranged for me to learn a valuable lesson.

During the first few months of my recovery, I was so sensitive to touch that every time someone just brushed by me accidentally, I overreacted by flinching very badly, scaring both myself and the other person. I attempted to explain that I was going through something that caused me to be hypersensitive. Then I could let it go and move on. But, when someone touched me purposely, such as to get my attention, their touch stayed with me for hours. My skin felt like an imprint had been made in a sponge and it took a long while to return to the original shape. For several times that this happened, I was not able to tell the person what was going on with me. The feelings of abuse and shame made me speechless, unable to stand up for myself.

Then one afternoon, as I was sitting, talking to a friend, a coworker walked up to me and pressed his hip into my arm to get my attention. Even though he had known about my sensitivity, he disregarded my feelings to satisfy his own needs. Once again I felt the imprint on my skin, but this time instead of shame, anger welled up inside of me. I turned to him and told him that he could never touch me in any way again. In that moment my boundary became firmly established. Now, I'm no longer afraid to speak up for myself. My sensitivity has lessened in the last few months, but it will always be there to some degree. My internal radar goes up whenever someone is around that I don't quite trust. I've become very comfortable in reaching to shake a person's hand when I feel that they are going for a hug. The people in my life that I trust the most are respectful of my needs and yes, I allow them to touch me and to give me my share of hugs. They affirm me in my growth in honoring my body. And, this sensitivity that I have to touch helps me to remember to be respectful of others' boundaries as well. There are times when I've been with a family during a crisis and everyone's emotions are running extremely high. An insensitive touch from someone could very easily push a person over the edge when they are so stressed. There are others that need touch during a critical time. I'm learning to use my instincts to discern when a caring touch is appropriate and when it isn't. When another person is in need of a hug or an arm around their shoulders, I'm able to put my needs aside for the moment because I know that I'm helping them by being compassionate and putting their feelings ahead of mine.

True Compassion

I had the privilege of being present to the most wonderful example of honoring another's body during one of my shifts at the hospital. A young woman was killed instantly in an automobile accident and was brought to our emergency room. The staff had paged for a chaplain to be there for the family when they arrived. As I waited for them, I stayed with the charge nurse and her staff has they cleaned the body of victim to ease her parents' suffering. I stood there watching in awe of the tenderness and the caring touches as blood was wiped away and glass removed. The girl's body was gently lifted and the soiled clothing was replaced with a hospital gown. Her long blond hair was brushed and laid over her shoulder to hide the damage to the side of her neck. I looked at the people caring for her and saw tears silently running down their faces as they grieved for this person that they did not know. I felt honored to be working alongside of such caring people. With tears in my eyes, I asked the staff if I could say a prayer for them. They bowed their heads as I thanked God for the gifts of compassion that He had given to each of them. I expressed my gratefulness in knowing them and for their willingness to let God work through them. We shared the Lord's Prayer together and they quietly went back to their work. After they had placed blankets on her body, one by one they left the room. Each looked back one final time at this beautiful body that they had carefully placed back together in order to care for the family that they would not meet. I had witnessed the ultimate act of unselfishness that God asks of each of us. Love one another as we love Him.

My Inner Voice

In the last few years, I have discovered that the most important way for me to honor my body in the way that God wants is by using my voice. When I entered the C.P.E. program, one of my goals was to find my inner voice and to share my thoughts and feelings in a way that others would respect. As a child I was told that children are to be seen and not heard. But, as I grew older that rule never seemed to go away. It was a tape that played over and over in my mind telling me that my opinions were worthless and no one would listen to me anyway. In order to achieve my goal in C.P.E., I first had to destroy that tape. My supervisor, Larry, helped me to do that by validating my thoughts when I had the courage to voice them. He encouraged me during class time by asking me what I was thinking. Over time, I began to be more comfortable in sharing my opinions. I started to believe that I did have something to say and that it was important. My education through C.P.E. has taught me how to have confidence in myself and to stand firm in my beliefs when challenged. I no longer run away or take on someone else's opinions if they are different from mine.

Having found my voice has given me the ability to honor myself when others don't. I have found strength that I didn't know existed within me to talk about the secrets in my childhood. The truth has been revealed to the family, and even though they cannot accept it, I have honored myself and God by exposing it. God has blessed me for my obedience by giving me a new freedom and peace that I've never known before.

I can't count how many times I have dishonored my body by allowing others to intimidate me. Every time I allowed the family to control me, I lost my self-respect. Whenever I gave in to someone's idea, even when I knew that mine was better, I devalued my confidence. If I ignored an instinct, I brought shame to my soul for not following God's word. That is not the life I wish to live any longer. God has given me many second chances to be who He intends for me to be. I will honor my body by surrendering my life to Him.

Body Reflections

Throughout our writing we have referred to God as "He." We realize that some may not be comfortable with this term. When Lori found a relationship with God she was looking for the loving compassionate father she never experienced as a child. Seeing God as her father has filled that void. God is always present, hearing her cries of distress even before she opens her mouth.

For Sara, God reminds her much of sitting on her Grandpa's lap. Since she was the oldest of seven children she does not remember sitting on either of her parents' laps. Her grandpa made her feel special. She felt connected without needing to say any words. His lap was a place of security and comfort. God has always provided a sense of security and comfort even though turbulence invaded her life.

Although we may not see God explicitly as a male, we are not uncomfortable addressing God as "He." In reality, God is neither he nor she. God is nonsexual. Our human language has provided no means of fully addressing our God. Just as it is difficult to describe the beauty of the sunlight causing the snow or water to look like diamonds, so it is when we attempt in our human language to describe God. Our deity is indescribable. Although we find difficulty in expressing who God is, we have discovered we can build an intimate relationship with our God and honor Him with our minds, bodies and souls.

As we reflect upon the importance and care of our body we are drawn to 1 Corinthians 6:19-20,

> *"Do you not know that your body is a temple of the Holy Spirit, who is in you, whom you have received from God? You are not your own you were bought at a price. Therefore honor God with your body."*

God dwells in our body and it is our responsibility to care for the house. We need to give our body the proper rest, nutrition and exercise. It is imperative that we keep our body in good condition, for God lives inside of us. We have taken the gift God has given us in these bodies off the shelf and we've studied, examined, held and loved them. There are many parts of our bodies that we wish we could change, but we've decided that this is who God had created and we will make the best of what He has given us. When we each learn how to honor our own bodies, then we can honor others. We long for the time to come when everyone treats each other with honor and respect. When that happens we will truly be honoring the Body of Christ, for that is what we are altogether. One magnificent body, whose only purpose is in praising our God.

Fuel for your journey

1. Which story caused you to think of your own experiences? Why?

2. How does it make you feel?

3. What would you like to say to God right now?

4. Who can you share these feelings with?

CHAPTER SEVEN

Hope
A New Vision

What does hopelessness look like to you? If you were to draw a picture of hopelessness, what would it look like? We think it would look like Eeyore, with his downcast eyes, drooping ears, head hanging low, tail dragging with a sad, piti-ful tone in his voice as he says, "Oh, bother!" Eeyore has given up and there's no purpose in his life. He exists day-to-day, waiting for the next bad thing to happen. And, guess what, bad things do happen to him.

If Eeyore is hopelessness, then who is hope? It's Pooh, of course! Pooh believes honey can be found anywhere if he only searches for it. He doesn't give up or get discouraged when he experiences difficulties. No matter what problems arise, he is always positive that he will find the honey. His positive out-look affects others, even Eeyore from time to time. What does

Pooh do when he runs into a jam? He yells, "Christopher Robin," because he knows that Christopher is available whenever he needs him. In the same way, God is available to us in our times of hopelessness.

Our world is full of Eeyores spreading their despair to others around them. All we need to do is turn on the evening news and we hear of wars, child abuse, murders, famines, forest fires and destruction. So how do we survive living in this Eeyore type of mentality? We search for hope in the midst of the sadness, knowing that we will find it just as Pooh finds his honey. In searching for our hope we may come upon roadblocks. Do we get discouraged and stop our search? Or do we call to God for help? Just as Christopher is always within hearing range of Pooh's call of distress, God is hearing our cry, too.

Lori

God's Serenade

As I reflect on my childhood and everything that I have remembered, I've tried very hard to discover what it was that helped me to keep the hope alive that things would get better. Why didn't I just give up? I wish that I could come up with someone or something that encouraged me to be myself and provided comfort for me. I know that I've always had a deep connection to music since I was very little. Songs could transport me into another world when I needed to escape. I remember listening to Dr. Doolittle and Mary Poppins albums over and over until the record was almost worn out. As I grew older I fell in love with singers like Donny Osmond, David Cassidy and especially Barry Manilow. When the arguments started at home, I would retreat to my bedroom and play my music. The songs I loved were ones about people in love. They gave me hope for the future.

As an adult, I enjoy many different kinds of music. I really like songs that have a message and ones that touch my heart.

Christian music has become my favorite in the last several years. These artists are able to take my feelings about God and put them in to words in order to praise Him. About the time of my first flashback, I bought the newest album by a popular Christian singer. His music has become part of my healing. Each song has touched me in a particular way. So many times I have felt alone in my pain and grief. Even with the support of those who love me, there is so much work that I need to do alone in order to heal completely. As much as Duane would like to take this suffering away for me, he knows and I know that he can't. It's in these times that he understands and gives me the time I need with my music. When I've lost my hope, I know that I will find it again in the center of the songs created for people who love God.

Maybe it was music that comforted me as a child in the same way it does now. I believe that God gave me a love for songs so that I would have something to turn to in the darkest moments. Something that would provide the hope I needed to face each day. As my recovery is continuing, the same songs that I turned to for hope, I turn to for validation and comfort that I am moving forward. I'm not in the same place I was just two years ago. My hope is built on nothing less than the song in my heart that God has created for me.

God's Ad Campaign

Knowing my love for music and the comfort that it brings me, God knew exactly how to reach me at a time when I was searching for Him, but didn't know where He was. This was the time when Margaret's cancer had taken over her body. I was literally watching her die before my eyes. Each day there was a difference in her eyes or her skin or her strength. Every moment with her became very precious and I would cry every time I left her. There were times, also, that I became angry. I had finally found the unconditional love I had longed for and God was taking it away from me.

During this transition in my life, I was working a few hours a week as the bookkeeper and receptionist at a hair replacement clinic. My relationship with the owner, Joan, and her assistant, Stacie, became very important to me. They are both spiritual, strong women and I believe now that God had placed them in my life to help me find my path to Him. Margaret had planted the seed, but Joan and Stacie were showing me how to care for it.

One morning at work I expressed my confusion and anger to Stacie about losing Margaret. I asked her to help me to understand why God would give me something that I needed and then take it away. Stacie began helping me to find answers by sharing scripture with me. She encouraged me to listen to Christian music and allow it to help me find peace. Joan shared stories of when her faith was all that kept her going after the death of her son. They wanted me to know that I could lean on God to help me survive Margaret's illness and her loss. But still I resisted.

I tried to follow Joan and Stacie's suggestions. While Margaret was resting, I sat in her den looking through her Bibles. The words seemed so confusing to me, though, that I would become frustrated and give up. I wanted so badly to talk to Margaret about this, but she was so weak and slept most of the time, I decided not to bother her with my concerns. When I was driving, I looked for the Christian radio station in our area. I would listen for a little while, but the songs meant nothing to me, so I turned it off.

Along with the grief of losing Margaret, Duane and I were also dealing with some financial problems. I knew that I needed to work full time, but my heart wanted to be with Margaret as much as I could. So we struggled, and the stress of it was building. I started to realize that everything I did was not working. I was losing control and felt defeated. There was nowhere for me to turn. I was ready to give up. My hope had slipped away from me. It was gone.

It was then that I began to notice something strange. Everywhere I drove, I was seeing bumper stickers on cars that advertised the local Christian Radio station that I had tried to listen to. When I pulled into a parking lot, the car in front of me had one. When I stopped for a traffic light, there it was again. Driving on the highway or the country roads where we live, every car ahead of me had the same bumper sticker. I actually became annoyed at all of these stickers. What right did that driver in front of me have to tell me to listen to his radio station?

One evening about a week later, I had just left the grocery store and headed home. My thoughts were circling from Margaret, to money, to finding a new job. My whole world was falling apart and I could do nothing to change it. I started crying, wondering what I was going to do and the image of the bumper sticker invaded my thinking. As I reached for the radio dial, I told myself I would listen one more time and that was it. No more. A song was playing about trusting God and when the chorus started about running to God, because His arms are open wide, I began crying heavily. It was as though all of my tears symbolized all of my lost dreams and hopes, my failures and my sadness. In that moment I knew that I could no longer do this alone and I asked God to help me. The song finished and my crying stopped. I didn't quite understand what had just happened, but inside I felt a difference. It was small and fragile, but it felt like hope again.

Slowly, things began to change in my life. It didn't happen instantly or overnight, but eventually it did. I began my walk to God with baby steps, feeling very wobbly and unsure. The radio station has become a part of my life and I listen all the time to hear that special song, but I have never heard it again. Stacie and Joan continued to teach me about the Bible and spirituality. A few months after Margaret died, I was able to find a full-time job and our finances have improved. I don't feel like a failure any longer. Even when I do make a mistake I try to learn from it and I allow God to pick me up again and put me back on the path. As my faith in Him has grown, my hope has become stronger. I now know that I can't have hope without faith. My faith allows my vision to be clear and on the watch for signs of God's love for me. The radio station's bumper stickers were used by Him to get my attention, and a special song that was sung especially for me gave me my hope back. What a wonderful gift, wrapped with beautiful people like Joan, Stacie and Margaret that contained my hope and faith—tied with the ribbon of the Holy Spirit to set everything in place. Just for me.

Sara
Communities of Hope

When I reflect upon the significant times of hope in my life I think of people offering hope and also finding hope in the Holy Scriptures. Community is important to me and God uses community to bring hope to my spirit.

When Les and I were in Recovery of Hope for our marriage, the last session we were to share with each other our dreams. I was so entangled with despair and feeling I needed to care for others that I had no dream for myself.

John, one of our therapists, suggested that I should pursue writing. When he mentioned writing it was like a thousand neon lights flashing. I now had a dream. For several years I wrote news articles for church publications and had a few stories published. I took several writing classes and attended a writer's conference. I was excited with my dream and focused much of my attention to help my dream become reality. A few years later I began working full time and lost the vision for writing. Sometimes Les would remind me that I should not forget about my writing, but I would reply that I was too busy.

My dream and the hope that had been vital to bringing change in my self-esteem lay dormant for more than fifteen years. Then, during the busiest time of my life God called Lori and me to write this book. There were no flashing neon lights this time, but rather a deep stirring in my spirit. There was no need for flashing lights, because I had learned to trust the nudges of the Holy Spirit.

It was like my hope had been a campfire with just a few embers left glowing when the breath of the Holy Spirit came and rekindled the flame. God has used the fifteen years to refine my character and bring to maturity those qualities that will allow my interactions with others to be more effective. Initially I used writing to escape from my husband; now my writing draws us closer to each other.

Surrender brought Hope

When we are given a new dream, hope or vision we have a desire to see it materialize immediately. We do everything in our power to make it happen now. God's ways are not our ways and often we are asked to maintain the vision while God does the work in His own time to bring the vision to reality. Even though it may take years, do not allow others to extinguish the hope that has been placed within your spirit.

It is often as we look back on experiences that we see God at work in our lives. Les and I attended a seminar concerning the Prayer of Jabez. This prayer is found in 1 Chronicles 4:10,

> *"Jabez cried out to God of Israel, 'Oh, that You*
> *would bless me and enlarge my territory! Let*
> *your hand be with me, and keep me from harm*
> *so that I will be free from pain.' And God*
> *granted his request."*

The speaker asked those who wanted God to enlarge their world, vision, and territory to come forward for prayer. I desired to go, but decided that I would not make a public decision without Les going forward with me. Without my saying anything to him, he reached over for my hand and asked if I wanted to go for prayer. We held each other close as we asked God to enlarge our vision.

This was the first time as a couple that we have been able to make a commitment of that level or depth. Our children are adults and have left home. Together, we told God we were open to whatever He had in mind for our lives. We had no idea what God would do. All we did was open ourselves to God's possibilities and dreams for us. We surrendered our egos to the Spirit of God, put aside our drive to achieve and allowed God to bring our hope to fruition. There is no hope without surrender.

Four years ago I attended my brother-in-law's installation as dean at Associated Mennonite Biblical Seminary. Sitting in the audience, I began dreaming of attending the seminary. I wanted to be in an environment of learning and growing. I had never attended college so I told myself it was not an attainable dream. But God placed a seed of hope in my spirit and then several years later, Larry, my C.P.E. educator, watered the seed. As I was in a supervision meeting with Larry, he mentioned that I may want to consider attending seminary. My immediate reply was that I would need to complete four years of college and that would make me almost sixty years old before I could begin.

I happened to mention the conversation to my sister and she suggested I speak with her husband. I discovered that the seminary is permitted to take 10 percent of their students without an undergraduate degree. My dream of attending seminary will become a reality this fall. God placed people in my pathway because God has plans for my life that involve my having a Master of Divinity degree. What the specific plans involve I have no idea. All that I know is that as I continue to remain open to the Spirit of God the way will be made clear.

Hope's Patchwork Quilt

As we remain open, God brings changes to our dreams. I believe nursing was part of God's plan for me, but now I'm beginning a new chapter in my life. As an expression of starting this new chapter and a sign of my trust in God, I felt it was important not to renew my nursing license. That chapter has been completed and a new chapter begun, which has yet to be completed. Hope prevails during this exciting adventure.

Has God forgotten about my husband, Les, as my hopes are being realized? As we began to see our plans being rearranged, Les struggled with how he would fit into this new direction. Some friends told us we were crazy because we should be planning for retirement rather than going to school. How did we know I would be able to get a job? I was being self-centered by taking my husband away from his work and friends. Les thought about the situation for several months and God gave him peace in the decision for me to go to school. It has been difficult for us to sell our home and especially his beautiful woodshop. God placed Les in contact with a camp that was looking for a maintenance person. The camp is only twenty miles from the seminary and he is doing work that he enjoys. God knows how to tend to each detail of our lives. My hope is centered upon the guidance of the Spirit of God.

Hope is energy—an energy that empowers and gives vitality. A prophet brought comfort to God's people in Isaiah 40:31,

> *"But those who hope in the Lord will renew*
> *their strength. They will soar on wings like*
> *eagles; they will run and not grow weary, they*
> *will walk and not be faint."*

When our hope is placed in God, rather than ourselves, we will experience an abundance of energy, beyond what others would expect. When my niece was diagnosed with cancer, and as she had chemotherapy, she kept the family informed through e-mail. Each communication was signed, "On Eagles Wings." She was aware of her source of strength. Throughout her battle with cancer she continued her college education. God provided remarkable strength and endurance for her.

Another verse from the Old Testament reminds us of our hope. We hear God's promise of hope in Jeremiah 29:11-14,

> *"I know the plans I have for you," declares the Lord, "plans to prosper you and not to harm you, plans to give you hope and a future. Then you will call upon me and come and pray to me, and I will listen to you. You will seek me and find me when you seek me with all your heart. I will be found by you," declares the Lord.*

God wants to give each of us hope. Ask God for that hope and reach out to the energy that will be supplied for you. God is faithful to His promises.

Lori
Labyrinth of Hope

On a beautiful July summer day, Sara and I were working on the book and became stuck. We were working on this chapter on hope. As we sat down to our computers we felt muddled and the words were not there for us to write. How do we tell someone about hope who has none? How do we write about our hope in God, if the person reading it does not know Him? How do we create a picture of hope? We didn't have much hope to write this chapter, so we did what we needed to do. We needed to spend time with God and wait on Him to provide us our answers.

Several months ago we had the opportunity to learn how to pray in a different way. This was to walk a labyrinth. In ancient times, labyrinths were designed into the floors of cathedrals in order for Christians to make a symbolic journey to Jerusalem when conflict in the Holy Land made it impossible for them to go there. The labyrinth is a series of pathways that eventually lead to the center. As you walk the paths, you embark on a spiritual journey of being quiet and waiting for God to speak to you. This tool has become a very powerful way for us to be with God. So when the answers would not come to us, we went to God.

Before we entered the pathways, Sara and I prayed to God to open our ears so that we could hear Him, to let the winds of the Spirit flow through us and to give us the words to write to tell others about Him. When we stepped onto the path, we each had our own individual experiences and messages from God. We spent our time in silence until we completed the labyrinth.

This labyrinth was formed into the landscape by planting of wildflowers and then mowing the path through it. We walked through the flowers and grass barefoot. The closer I came to the middle of the labyrinth the grass under my feet felt like thick carpeting. As I walked back and forth, through the winding path, I reached out to touch the grass and the flowers alongside of me. I stopped several times and picked a flower that caught my attention. The sun was shining brightly and the wind tossed my hair as I walked on towards the center.

I felt as though I was walking on Holy Land as I carefully made my way. I repeated my question of hope over and over again in my mind, until at last I reached the center of the labyrinth. I sat down on the ground and carefully held each of the flowers I had picked. God helped me to see how the flowers were like me. Some were tall and strong and others tiny and fragile. One flower had pulled out by the root when I picked it and as I laid it in front of me I remembered that God knows every part of me, from roots to blossom. There was a beautiful orange flower that made me smile when I looked at it. This flower represented my sense of humor. Another was a blossom that had withered and looked ugly, but when I looked inside of it, there were beautiful seeds waiting to be scattered. This was the side of me that held the secret of my abuse, even after I became aware of it, but inside was the hope for a better future waiting to escape.

I carefully arranged the flowers on the ground into a bouquet to place before God. As each of the flowers symbolized a different part of me, it was myself that I was laying before Him. I sat there looking at the bouquet for a while, in awe of how they all came together so beautifully. Even the buds that had died looked pretty next to the ones in full bloom. Once again I asked God my question. How do I tell others about hope? It was then that He answered me;

> *When there is hope...God is there.*
>
> *When you hope that the flowers will bloom...*
> *God is there.*
>
> *When you fall asleep at night and hope to wake*
> *in the morning...God is there.*
>
> *When you hope that your children are*
> *healthy...God is there.*
>
> *When you hope that the pain of suffering will*
> *end...God is there.*
>
> *When you hope to see your loved one again after*
> *death...God is there.*
>
> *When you hope to find the answers...*
> *God is there.*

God had answered my questions. Hope is, knowing that God is always there and life goes on. Where I had picked the flowers, new ones will grow, blossom, die and the cycle will continue. Even though many of my flowers represented the hard times that I've been through, I can have the hope that my life will be as beautiful as the arrangement I had created and placed before God.

As I stood then in the middle of the labyrinth, I felt the warmth of Jesus in the sun on my face and the freedom of the Spirit in the wind blowing through me. I turned in a circle, and everywhere I stopped, the warmth and the wind were still there. I knelt before my bouquet on the ground and bowed to God in gratitude. Slowly, I left the center and made my way back out of the labyrinth taking the same path as I had going in. At one of the turns, I noticed a beautiful yellow butterfly leaving the labyrinth at the same time. I watched as it flew off to lands unknown and felt my spirit soar side by side with it.

Sara

The beauty and depth of the labyrinth could not be appreciated as we stood on the outside. In searching for our answer we began with slow purposeful steps toward the center. The grasses were tall, almost to our waist and our hands gently caressed the seeds waltzing in the wind.

The wind reminded me of the Spirit and in the warmth of the sun I saw God shining upon us with pleasure. As I strolled through the path I noticed the intricate beauty of a large dandelion-type of seed. As I examined the seed and held it between my fingers I was impressed with the delicate and fragile design of seed. The tail glistened in the sun, representing for me the attractiveness of hope. Initially our hope may appear to be fragile but as the wind of the Spirit blows upon it, hope is able to travel many miles touching the lives of others.

Walking through the paths I saw beetles and bugs eating the plants. A few prickly weeds grew among the flowers. Even though these were present, the flowers continued to bloom and display their colors. I could have chosen to either focus on the predators or the flowers, the choice was mine. I chose to see the elegance of the plants.

As I was sitting in the center of the labyrinth I recalled my writing concerning the connection of hope and surrender. As a demonstration of my surrender to God, I lay on the grass telling God that I was made of the earth and that is all I was until He breathed into me the breath of life. In myself, I can find no hope, for my hope comes only from God.

When I sat up I began searching around the plants and discovered some stones. These stones were not easily seen, I needed to search for them. Sometimes that is how hope is; we need to look for it. When I found the rocks it changed my vision of the labyrinth. They were firm and provided a foundation, just as a new vision provides for us a foundation upon which we can build our hopes and dreams. Dreams are the hopes that can change a person's life, give them a new vision and the courage to move forward. However, one cannot make a hope turn into a reality on only hope alone. We need faith. Faith is what is needed to keep the hope alive when everything else tries to crush it.

Hopeful Reflections

Jarius, a synagogue leader, had a desperate need. His young daughter was dying. He had the hope that Jesus would be able to heal his daughter. He approached Jesus as a broken father, pleading that Jesus would come to his house and touch her body. Jesus began to follow Jarius to his home.

The father's hope increased with each step taken that brought them closer to home. Many people were milling about them and suddenly Jarius heard Jesus ask, "Who touched me?" Jarius thought, "Why does He need to know who's touching Him? I have people touching me too in this crowd. What's the deal? Let's get moving, my daughter is dying." Jarius felt that Jesus wasted precious moments healing a woman who had touched him.

While this was happening, Jarius' friends informed him that his daughter had died. They added, "Don't bother Jesus because all hope of healing for your daughter is gone."

Jarius felt his heart drop to his feet. Hope was so close and now it was gone. Tears filled his eyes and he began to turn away from Jesus in despair. But Jesus turned to him and said, "Don't be afraid; just believe." They continued to walk to Jarius' home.

When they arrived, the people that had gathered were crying and wailing. Jarius wanted to believe Jesus, but this was too much for him to handle. As they entered the house Jesus told the mourners that the child was not dead, but only sleeping. They laughed in disbelief at His comment.

Jesus asked all the people to leave the room. Only Jarius, his wife and several disciples were present. As they gathered around the mat, Jesus reached out and took the child's hand and asked her to get up. Jarius watched in amazement as his daughter stood to her feet and began walking.

Like Jarius, we also need to wait until our dreams are realized. Interruptions may seem to interfere with our plans. This is when we really need to be patient, hang onto our dream and wait. God will provide in the appropriate time as we place our trust in God's provision.

Jesus surrounded Himself with the people that had faith and were hopeful. This is how we find our hope; we surround ourselves with hopeful people. When our hopes are realized, many will be surprised, but we will know the truth. Faith is what allowed our hopes and dreams to come true.

Fuel for your journey

1. Which story caused you to think of your own experiences? Why?

2. How does it make you feel?

3. What would you like to say to God right now?

4. Who can you share these feelings with?

CHAPTER EIGHT

Relationships

Building Love Bridges

Deep in a forest in California where large trees called sequoias grow, a very inspirational event is happening everywhere. If you could look at the inside of the earth, below the trees, you would see a community of networking taking place. Every tree in the forest is in relationship to another. The roots are intertwined so tightly that it's almost impossible to separate them. Whatever the trees need to survive they share with each other, the warmth of the sunshine, the life-sustaining rain and the nutrients from the soil. This is how the trees are able to flourish, grow tall and strong. By working and living together, all benefit.

We as a people could learn a lot from these trees. Imagine a world where all are working together for one good. There would be no separation of those who have and those who have not. Is it possible? Maybe, but we have a lot of work to do to make it happen. Creating relationships is the very first step.

Relationship building is hard work. It takes time, patience and commitment to learn how to relate to someone in a healthy way. Just as building a bridge is slow and meticulous, so it is with relationships if we want to build something that will be strong, safe and link us to others. For that is how we could grow a community like the sequoias. It takes reaching out to others, taking the risk and caring about each other. Once the connections are made, we are able to share what we've learned with all to build a strong network that can in turn reach out to more and more people until at last we have constructed a bridge of love. This is the kind of love that can change a world into a community that flourishes and benefits all.

Sara

My Tapestry

I was taking my morning walk after a night of rain. The cloudless sky was cobalt blue and the moisture on the leaves glistened like diamonds. The birds sang and all was at peace in my world. This is the picture I have of the relationships I have built over the years. They have added color and beauty to my life. The relationships I've developed, in many ways, define who I am as a person. Through relationships my world has been broadened and I'm more complete as a result of the people who have influenced my life.

In many aspects I'm a tapestry created by God in a unique manner. There is no other tapestry like mine because of the relationships I've had. Each person has added his or her individual thread of color and texture to God's creation. The beauty of the tapestry is in the diversity of relationships.

As I reflect upon my process of relationship building, I discover that as I've matured, my relationships have become deeper and more meaningful. As a young person I built relationships only for the present situation, my school friends and teachers. These tended to be superficial and did not have much commitment.

When I married Les I made a commitment that I would remain in relationship with him until we are separated by death. I did not realize the magnitude of that commitment until we had trouble in our marriage. We both chose to work diligently at our relationship so it could be reborn and strengthened. As a result of our choice I have learned to persevere to trust God with my life and that love is more than a feeling; it is a choice. Les has added a dimension to my life that would have been a huge void if we had not married. I have discovered I'm a stronger woman than I thought and have gifts and abilities that were lying dormant. Les and I enjoy doing fix-up projects together, hiking, biking and cross-country skiing. We have developed a feeling of comfortableness and companionship. We provide security and a sense of belonging for each other. We are in relationship.

My first full-time employment after I graduated from high school brought forth an interesting relationship. The manager at the gift shop was a compassionate man in his mid thirties. He was going through a divorce and seeking relationships like myself. He was the first male that affirmed me as a female and encouraged me to make myself more attractive. I "fell in love" with him. I dreamed of caring for him and his five-year-old daughter. I would take his daughter with me when I made deliveries to other gift shops in the evening. After two years I chose to leave his employment because I felt the relationship was wrong. Thirty-five years later I met the daughter at a social event and we both knew that we had connected previously. After a few moments we realized she was the little girl I had taken with me when working at the gift shop. We both had a warm feeling knowing that God had brought us together again. Relationships become very intertwined just as the roots of the sequoias.

Threads of Pain

I believe God brings particular people into our life to benefit them and also us. Soon after I was married I had the opportunity to work as a home nurse for a physician who had suffered a stroke. He and his wife were not able to have children and they had few extended family. That summer his wife and I became very close. She provided for me intellectual stimulation because she enjoyed talking about books and ideas. After he died we adopted her into our family. She celebrated Christmas with us and we often had lunch together. When we had our first Christmas as a family in Michigan, we had trouble feeling the joy of the holidays without our special auntie. During a visit she mentioned that her husband had told her that I was the daughter they were never able to have.

Auntie was living in a cottage at a retirement community. After an extensive hospitalization I worked hard to have her return to her cottage with nursing care, which was her desire. I returned to Michigan and kept in touch with telephone calls. It soon became apparent her health was not improving and I again flew to Pennsylvania. Her trust officer provided the finances to make my travel possible. He asked if I was aware of her will and told him only that she said she was leaving me a little "nest egg." I discovered through him that I was not mentioned in her will. She had left her money to organizations. I was hurt and angry. Not so much because of the money, rather what I felt it said about our relationship. Our family and a cousin were the only ones to attend her burial service. I grieved over the loss of Auntie and what felt to me like the loss of relationship. To bring healing I went through her old photo albums and removed pictures of her childhood, found a love letter her husband had written to her while he was in medical school and added pictures we had taken of activities with her. As I arranged them in a new album, I recalled the gift of relationship we had shared that did not depend on money. The stories of her childhood became more real to me with these pictures and I was able to remember the good times we had shared together. Interwoven in this thread continues to be some disappointment and pain.

Golden Threads

A special thread that runs through my tapestry is a friend I learned to know when I worked for her parents. She was my age and paraplegic since birth. We developed a relationship because we both needed a friend. After work I would lie on her bed, and she would share with me the latest happenings of "Days of Our Lives." Later we enrolled in a craft-a-month club and together we shared the joy of creating a work of art. Even after my daughters were born I spent time with her on a monthly basis when I helped her mother with part of her healthcare. My daughters learned not to think it was strange to see a person in a wheelchair. When they crawled, she would laugh, as they would use her wheels to pull themselves into a standing position. In her forties, she was diagnosed with cancer and I continued my visits. One afternoon when I drove by her house I felt drawn to stop. As I entered, her dad informed me she had just died. He asked if I would go back to her room and spend time with her mother. We touched her body, stroked her hair and spoke of the memories and gifts this daughter and friend had given to us.

Some relationships we initiate, and in others we are approached by a person seeking a relationship with us. Within several months of attending a new church, a young woman returning to the community, after college and a year of mission work, asked me if I would consider being her mentor. I had been mentored by an older woman, but had never been asked formally to be a mentor. I felt honored and we began meeting on a weekly basis during her lunch hour. She shared with me the disappointment of a relationship that ended and then we waited together for God to bring a more suitable young man into her life. It was a joy to be the wedding coordinator and share in their celebration of love. After we moved to Michigan we shared long distance in the trials and joys of the adoptions of their daughters. We don't often connect but there is a bond that distance will not destroy.

Family Threads

Family provides a colorful variation in my tapestry. My parents have been present for me since birth. Even though at times we did not agree, they were supportive of me. They gave me love and as an adult I appreciate their faith and openness to the leading of God in their lives. My six siblings have intertwined in my life in a variety of ways. Growing up we shared many childhood events. Because we have our own families we seldom connect except on holidays and our annual family gathering at Charter Hall. These are happy times of celebration as we share our most recent dreams and adventures. Heidi and Heather, our daughters, have taught me what it means to be a mother. Heidi challenged me with her strong will and desire to be independent. In many ways Heather was just the opposite, desiring to be close emotionally and physically. As adults they have gifted me with the love of a mother-daughter relationship. Being a grandma has added a new joy as I marvel at the development of our grandson and respond to his endless energy.

Multicolored Threads

The international acquaintances I had as a child helped me in developing relationships with the international doctors and their families. The texture these relationships have brought to my life has been satisfying and exhilarating. I have learned to enjoy eating their foods, exploring their religious beliefs and understanding their cultural backgrounds. I helped them to adapt to the American culture and in turn they opened the door for me to connect with their world. I hold this gift close to my heart and will always treasure their friendships.

Threads of Community

Woven through these individual relationships are two organizations, Recovery of Hope and Moms In Touch International. In seeking the help and therapy that Recovery of Hope provided, I connected to a husband and wife team. As therapists, they provided a safe environment to share my feelings and helped me to begin to believe in myself. They opened the possibility of learning to write. Through their encouragement, I discovered I could travel a different path and thought pattern than I had been feeding into my mind. As a result of my involvement with Moms In Touch International, I developed my leadership skills, and most important, I built relationships with other mothers as we prayed for our children and their schools. With these women I shared my rawest emotions while experiencing love and acceptance. My children became their children and their children became mine as we brought them before God, asking that He intervene in their lives. Gathering with these women has enhanced my vision of prayer. As I focus on the character of God, I believe God is sovereign and has only the best in mind for His creation. God's plans hold no mistakes.

Risking Relationships

The C.P.E. program provided many opportunities to build relationships with patients, peers, staff and educator. It was in this setting I learned through some difficult experiences. I was assigned to the cancer support group to meet their spiritual needs. From the previous chaplains I learned that the social worker with whom I would work did not allow the chaplain to do much. I went the first week and decided to agree with my peers' evaluation. I chose to discuss the situation as a case study. After I fussed and fumed about how I felt like I was the social worker's puppet, Urias asked how much time I had spent getting to know the social worker. I guessed it may have been five minutes or less. I was encouraged to have lunch with him and learn to know him as a person, in other words, build a relationship. I took the risk and the relationship spread throughout the support group. When I was facilitating the group I became vulnerable by sharing some of my struggles and dreams. Before the meeting was over several others felt free to share some heavy burdens they were carrying. We connected as a group because I was willing to take the risk of building a relationship.

Not always do our efforts of relationship-building meet with success. Again it was in the C.P.E. setting that my relationship-building was tested. Urias was attending a meeting and we were having difficulties getting along as a group of four chaplain residents. The conflict was a power struggle issue between two members. The other two were affected by the dynamics and felt uncomfortable. We could feel that an explosion was about to happen so we attempted to begin talking about the situation. We were careful not to blame and gave "I" messages, instead of "you" messages. Our efforts were futile and the explosion occurred.

We were a muddled mess when Urias arrived and we gave him a short summary of our efforts to resolve the situation. Instead of giving us an answer to our dilemma, he helped us to explore what was happening. It was decided that the conflict was like a tiger in the room. He asked each to describe what the tiger looked like. We all had a different image of the animal. For one the tiger was growling, another saw an injured animal, for another the tiger was a female protecting her cubs and still another focused on the tiger's sharp teeth. We each had our own perception of the tiger. The more we learned about the tiger the less frightening it became. The same is true of difficult relationships. The more authentic honest interaction we have with a person, the greater the possibility of developing a healthy meaningful relationship. These types of relationships take patience, skill and unselfish love.

My tapestry is by no means complete. There are many more threads to be added and only God knows the complete design. God is the weaver and I have the opportunity to enjoy and benefit through the skill of a master weaver.

Lori

Mutuality

A few years ago, while sitting in class at the Lay Ministry program, I heard a word that I had not heard before, *mutuality,* which is to have a relationship that is based on mutual respect. I learned that it's possible to disagree with someone and yet, the relationship can remain strong. Until that moment, I had thought that in order to have a bond with someone, I needed to always agree with the other person. Since I was taught that my opinions did not matter, this is how I learned to relate to others. The result is that I've allowed myself to be controlled and used for many years.

As I listened to the instructor speaking about healthy relationships, I began to cry. I realized that mutuality was something that I had been searching for my whole life. This helped me to understand that the things happening within the family at the time were not my imagination, it was me searching for something better. My tears represented the gratefulness I felt for having my feelings validated by someone. There was also a sense of sadness at having lived this way for nearly forty years, when my relationships could have been so much more fulfilling.

Now that I had learned what I needed, I wondered how I would begin creating bonds that were based on mutuality. I started by looking at the people around me. My classmates at the Diocese all treated each other with respect and I found that my thoughts and opinions were welcomed and accepted. I watched, listened and learned as they were teaching me and yet they didn't realize it. They were only being themselves and I was soaking in this knowledge like a sponge.

My new skills helped me to begin relating to others in the same ways. My co-workers and family began to notice the difference in me. Some family members did not like the ways I had changed since it upset their "normal" way of handling things. My relationship with myself has given me the wisdom, courage and strength to withstand the family's comments and stand firm. My bonds with those that affirmed the changes in me have deepened considerably. They have become my strongest supporters and encouragers.

Healthy, Loving Relationships

Two of these people are my husband's parents, Duane and Barb. In the twenty-six years that I've known them, our relationships have grown as well as my respect for them. I remember the first time I met Duane's family. The difference between our families was very apparent. The moment I walked through the door, I felt very welcome and I enjoyed being with them. It was like a breath of fresh air and I was relaxed and comfortable.

We had arrived just in time for dinner, and Duane and his brother Brian helped their mom bring the food to the table. One time as they came through the kitchen door, Duane was carrying his mom over his shoulder and Brian was pushing them along. They were laughing hysterically as she jokingly yelled at them to put her down. I remember wondering how I had landed into such a goofy family; it was crazy, strange and felt like a real home.

My relationship with them has not been a typical in-law one. We became close in the beginning and in the last few years have only strengthened the bond that was there. There are many in-law jokes and none of them would apply to mine. They respect us enough to make our own decisions; we help each other and really enjoy being together. I consider Duane and Barb to be my mom and dad.

When I took the first steps in my journey to becoming a chaplain, I received support and encouragement from each of them. They understood when I was busy studying and working long hours. At the end of my first unit of C.P.E., there was a graduation ceremony and I had to say good-bye to my peers that were leaving. I had been accepted into the residency program, which would start in just ten days with all new people. It was hard to let my support system that had been with me for the summer leave. I wasn't sure what I would do without them. After several hugs and a tearful farewell to all, I left the hospital and went to Mom and Dad's house to show them my certificate.

Mom had planned a small celebration for me with gifts and a card. As I sat on their front porch, the emotions of the day overwhelmed me. I put my head in my hands and cried. I was thinking about how hard it was going to be to walk back into work and start new relationships all over again. There were also thoughts of all the patients and families that I had been with in the last ten weeks. Within that time I had been present at the deaths of over forty people and had held their loved ones as they grieved. Some of those that died had been children and I was still grieving for them in my heart. So I cried. The tears wouldn't seem to stop. Then I felt an arm around my shoulders and heard Dad say to me, "You go ahead and cry, you've been through a lot this summer." I needed to hear those words, especially from my father. It wasn't long before I felt a little better and we continued our celebration. Dad had reached out to me and connected in a way that strengthened me. He was able to do that because of the relationship that we have and our respect for each other.

Even though my mother-in-law and I have always been close, since I found my way back to God, a new spiritual bond has been created between us. As Mom has shared her faith with me, I've been able to see another dimension of her that I couldn't see before because I was lacking in faith. Now we share books, music and discussions of the Bible. Because our relationship has gone to a deeper level, Mom seems to know when I need encouragement, hugs and her famous brownies. She is so proud of my work as a chaplain and she is the only one that I'll let call me "Chappie." Whenever we are together and she introduces me to someone, I am her daughter, the chaplain.

A couple of years ago on Christmas Eve, Duane, the kids and I attended church with Mom and Dad. They belong to a Presbyterian church and the service we went to was the children's pageant. It was wonderful. As the celebration came to a close, we began putting our coats on to leave. Dad quickly took my hand and said, "Let's go." I wondered why we were hurrying toward the back of the church, passing people on the way and then I understood. There was a line of people waiting to speak to the minister on their way out. Dad took me to the front of the line and introduced me to him. He told the minister that I was working at the hospital as a chaplain. As I was shaking his hand, Mom came up from behind and said to Dad, "Did you tell him that she's a chaplain?" I couldn't help but giggle at them. After speaking to the minister for a few moments, we left the church. As we drove to Mom and Dad's house to open presents, I realized that I had already been given a gift from them. Their gift was their pride and the opportunity to be part of a relationship with two wonderful people.

Hidden Treasure

Part of creating a new relationship with someone is finding a connection with them. Sometimes this is difficult to do, but by asking questions and actively listening you will find something in common. It could be anything such as children the same age, having gone on a vacation to the same place, pets, etc. Once the connection is found, it becomes the foundation on which a relationship can be built. This has happened many times to me in my work at the hospital. Finding that connection is like searching for treasure. You can't rely on a map to get you there, you have to use your instincts and watch for clues. A lot of times, the treasure will never be found, but when it is, it becomes a time of celebration in having made a new friend.

Often I will make a connection with a patient as we pray together. During our conversation, I listen intently for the things that the person cares about. When the time comes for the prayer, I am connected to the patient by the words I pray from my heart. This makes the prayer very personal and special for them. We become part of a holy moment together.

One day I was called to the outpatient surgery waiting area to see a thirteen-year-old girl who was going to have her gallbladder removed. Her parents had requested that someone come and pray. I introduced myself to them as I arrived and then turned my focus to the patient. We chatted for a few minutes and she answered my questions about school, hobbies, etc. Then I asked her what was the worst thing about being sick.

"Not being able to eat what I like," she said, "like pizza and hamburgers."

"How long has it been since you've had pizza?" I asked.

"At least a month or so, it's been a real long time," she told me.

I agreed with her that a month was way too long to go without pizza. She also told me that she had missed a lot of school and she missed her friends. My next question for her was if she was afraid of the surgery.

She looked at me with sad eyes and said, "I'm afraid I won't wake up when it's over." Her parents explained that they had been assuring her that the doctor would give her medicine to help her wake up, but she was still worried.

"Lisa, would it be okay with you if I asked God to take away your fear?" She nodded. "Okay," I said, "let's pray." She bowed her head and folded her hands together. I began, "God, Lisa is very worried today about not waking up after the surgery. I ask You to let her know that You are here and that she can relax and not be afraid. We know that the doctors are very smart and they know exactly what to do to wake her up. Father, I also ask You to be with Lisa's parents as they wait to see her after the surgery. And, God, please help Lisa to get better very quickly so that she can enjoy spending time with her friends and eating pizza again. I pray these things in Jesus' name. Amen."

I looked up and she was smiling. "Thank you," she said, "that was cool!" Her mom and dad were laughing with her. The time came for her to go to the operating room, but before she left she asked me if I would come and see her when she woke up. I promised I would be there. The surgery went very well and the nurse paged me when Lisa was waking up. I went to see her. When she opened her eyes, I smiled at her and said, "Hey Lisa, you're awake." She was still very sleepy, but she said, "Cool," again and asked me to tell her parents.

I had found my treasure during my visit with Lisa. We made a connection over pizza and a prayer. She went home later that day. I may not see her again, but our friendship is preserved forever, in our hearts.

Breaking the Ties

There are times when being in a relationship with someone becomes stale, one-sided or harmful to us. It's a hard process to go through to discern if the time has come to cut ties with the person. Sometimes relationships can be renewed if both parties are willing to put in the work. It can't be saved, however, if only one person is trying. Doing this is like butting your head up against a brick wall to break through. The wall will not come down and you'll end up severely harming yourself.

The end of a relationship can be as difficult and painful as the death of a loved one and in some ways even greater since the person is still here, within reach, but not willing to be reached. The grief may be very intense and overwhelming, especially since the loss usually involves several people that are connected within the relationship. But, do we stay in a relationship that's dying in order to preserve the other's feelings at the expense of our own? Where do we create the boundaries? How do we stop letting others use us in the name of relationship?

These questions and more have been part of my decision to stop allowing the family to control me. I began doing this by placing boundaries on our relationships. As a result, the ties have been broken. I didn't wish this to happen, but I knew in my heart that it would. My attempts to be open and honest about the abuse I've remembered have pushed them further away from me. Even though the odds were extremely good that this is what would happen, I still had a tiny bit of hope inside that someone would come forward and support me. Since that hasn't happened, I am grieving the loss of that hope and the relationships with my siblings and parents. Within the grief is a great deal of anger at them for not caring about me. There are times when I'm immersed in the pain of realizing that my feelings were not considered as a child and are still ignored as an adult.

It's hard for me to imagine a parent that does not care about their child. The relationship that I have with Jase and Krystina is strong enough that I can sense when something is wrong. It may be their tone of voice or body language. Sometimes it's just my maternal instinct that sends up my radar. When they are hurting I would give my life to take away their pain. Nothing could keep me from them. If I'm the one who has hurt them somehow, I want to know, so I can make it right again.

This is not true of my parents. They know that the memories I've had have revealed that I was sexually abused. During my last conversation with my mother, I told her that I was hurting. Her response was to accuse me of wanting to hurt others because of it. What I wanted was my mother to help me and to take away some of the pain. She is not capable of doing that. As for my dad, there has been nothing. No contact of any kind. I have become non-existent in their lives.

So I feel as if the family has died. Yet, there were no funerals, no chance to say good-bye and no closure. For the most part, I am better since I'm not involved with them any longer. I feel a freedom that I'd never had before. The relationships had been suffocating me and had almost murdered my soul. But, God saved me. My commitment to Him is so vital to my life that I could recognize when the family's control was keeping me from Him. Finally, I came to a point of surrendering to Him rather than the family. This is when the relationships crumbled.

But, there is that part of me that grieves heavily for what I've lost. The little girl inside of me cries for her mom and dad to take care of her, just as she did when I was small. It's that child that can't understand what has happened. She feels abandoned and alone. The abuse has not ended in her life, it continues.

Now, it's up to me to protect her. I have taken her away from the situation. She no longer has to face those who abuse her. Slowly, she has learned to trust again. Together we are building relationships with our family of choice. As she finds the people she can depend on to be there for her, she is finding the freedom to be herself. God has restored her and given back the innocence that was taken from her. I am whole again. I am His child.

Intertwining Reflections

The skill of building relationships can best be shown through the life of Jesus. His interaction with a Samaritan woman as she was coming to Jacob's well to draw water is a very moving story. It was noontime and a woman was coming alone to the well. Because she did not come with the other village women it was apparent that her community did not accept her.

Jesus approached her by asking her for a drink of water. She was surprised, because Jewish men did not speak with Samaritan women. Jesus pursued the relationship as they discussed His ability to give her water so she would never need to come to the well again. After He had developed a rapport with her, He asked for some personal information. He asked to meet her husband. His following comments were nonjudgmental as He revealed to her that He knew of her martial situation. She perceived Him to be a prophet, so she asked a religious type of question. Jesus took the opportunity to explain to her that true worship is not about a place, rather worship happens within the spirit. She made little connection to that comment, but a friendship had been established between them and she returned to the village to tell others to come and meet this prophet.

Jesus' followers were shocked to find Him speaking with a Samaritan woman. Because Jesus took the time to build a relationship with a most unlikely person He was able to spend two days in the village teaching. He accepted her as a person, of value and in turn, He had the opportunity to build relationships with an entire village (John 4).

This story challenges us to approach relationship building with skill, persistence, gentleness and an open spirit. God uses some unlikely people to enhance our tapestry of relationships.

In Matthew 23, the Pharisees, who were the religious leaders in Jesus' time, came to see Him again. They did not agree with His teachings and tried to discredit Him with the people. In the first verse of the chapter, Jesus talks about the Pharisees as people who preach God's word, but do not practice it. The Pharisees lived by the laws of their traditions and the Bible, yet they failed to recognize Jesus for who He was, the Messiah.

Jesus' love for all included the Pharisees and it hurt Him to know that they did not believe in Him. Many times He tried to build a relationship with them by being honest and telling them the truth of God's love, but their narrow vision kept them from recognizing Him. Jesus was not able to make a connection with them in the way that He had hoped. They made assumptions about Him and tried to make others believe that He was a liar and an imposter.

Shortly before Jesus died, He made one last attempt to help the Pharisees see themselves as God sees them. Over and over, He pleaded with them to listen. But, they would not hear Him. They turned their backs and walked away, leaving Him to grieve for them. Within a few days, they would turn Jesus over to Pilate to be crucified.

This passage from Scripture shows us how much God loves us. Our relationship with Him is our treasure. Jesus proved that no matter how many times the Pharisees turned their backs on Him and walked away, He still loved them. But, even Jesus understood that some people are not able or willing to be in a relationship. He accepted the fact that the bridge that

He wanted to build to connect the Pharisees with God was not possible in His lifetime. It took His death to complete it.

As relationships come and go in our lives, due to the changes and circumstances we all have, there is one bridge that will always be there. The one which links us to God. No matter how many times we turn away from God, He is always there waiting for us to turn around again. We can trust that the bridge of love that Jesus built with His cross is strong and everlasting. This is a relationship that will last for eternity.

Fuel for your journey

1. Which story caused you to think of your own experiences? Why?

2. How does it make you feel?

3. What would you like to say to God right now?

4. Who can you share these feelings with?

CHAPTER NINE

Soul Connections
The Braid of Life

Soul connections are very precious relationships that we experience in our lives. They are deep connections that become embedded in our souls. These relationships are like the pearl, a gem of great value. The process of the oyster creating a pearl is one of struggle and perseverance, much like the work that God asks us to do to discover a treasure within another person.

As oysters siphon water over their gills for oxygen to breathe, they also strain out organic food particles. Occasionally a piece of food becomes lodged in an oyster's tissue. The small "food" creature struggles to free itself until eventually it dies and is entombed within the oyster. During the struggle, the food creature breaks through the oyster's mantle and takes a piece of this tissue with it. It continues to grow and soon it surrounds the food creature, forming a pocket called the pearl sack. This will eventually become the center of the pearl. To protect the oyster's tissue from the foreign body, the cells of the pearl sack secrete layer upon layer of nacre, which is made of minerals and proteins. This results in the creation of a natural pearl.

Our soul connections develop in somewhat the same manner. In the daily activities of life we occasionally "breathe" in a person that becomes entombed within our being. Sometimes there will be a struggle because we may not want to allow the person to become that close. But, during the struggle we allow this person to know who we really are. As the relationship continues to develop, the Spirit forms a pocket around the bond. The Spirit becomes the center of the relationship. The bond between the two is based on the Spirit, not personality or commonality. The Spirit protects this relationship as it forms, so a natural pearl of great beauty develops.

Our Story

In order for the two of us to become the pearl that God intends us to be, He needed to intertwine us with the Spirit to form a braid of closeness and strength. Because we were not confident in our discernment of following the Spirit, He chose the skillful hands of Urias to gently support the braiding process. It didn't take long for Urias to become one of our soul connections. As the Spirit became braided with ours, we needed affirmation from Urias that we were on the right path. In time, our faith became stronger, the braid became tighter with the Spirit and we felt a new confidence in ourselves that we had never had before.

This process caused us to struggle and go through a lot of pain. In the beginning, we found it difficult to open our souls to each other. This was a result of the pain of the former supervisor leaving. We had been deeply hurt and we were determined not to become vulnerable again, only to be disappointed. We remained hard and rigid, not willing to be flexible. The combination of his wisdom and listening to the Spirit allowed Urias to be very patient with us.

After Urias suffered a stroke, we were able to take a long hard look at ourselves. We were surprised at how much we had come to care about him, and it softened our hearts. Several weeks later, as we watched a C.P.E. video, the concluding segment presented Urias sharing a story of receiving Grace. He spoke of a time when he knew he had made a huge mistake during a counseling session with a client. His supervisor called him to the office and Urias was ready to be reprimanded. When he arrived, they sat and chatted for a while and then the supervisor told him that was all. As Urias was leaving, thinking that his mistake had not been noticed, the supervisor told him one more thing, that he would make a counselor out of him yet. In that moment, Urias received Grace. He went on to say that Grace is like a ball rolling around in the room unnoticed, until someone has the courage to pick it up and throw it to another in need of Grace.

We replayed the segment several times with tears in our eyes as we realized that Urias had already thrown us the ball of Grace. Our hearts opened and we allowed Urias to show us how to become braided with the Spirit. This has been the beginning of a new life for us. We no longer fear the Spirit, but feel the strength in being part of this braid of life. For God's word tells us in Ecclesiastes 4:12,

"A cord of three strands is not quickly broken."

When we least expected it, God offered us His Grace. Our relationship with Urias has been braided into a beautiful, long-lasting soul connection by the skillful hands of God.

Lori
Tommy and Dorothy

The soul connections that I have been blessed with in my life resulted during times of needing someone to support me. These were the darkest moments of my life, when I felt very alone. As I searched and reached out, God provided what I needed from Him in others. When I was little and afraid, He allowed my imagination to comfort me. This gift became my very first soul connections, Tommy and Dorothy, my imaginary friends.

Many children have imaginary friends in their early years. This is a completely normal part of childhood. Eventually, as the child grows, the need for the friends diminishes and finally disappears. I believe this was the reason for me "finding" Tommy and Dorothy in the beginning, but as the abuse was occurring I became dependent on them to be there for me. Their presence was the support I needed to survive. They provided the comfort I so desperately needed, but wasn't receiving. I don't remember what my imagination had created them to look like, but I do know that they were children also. During one of my first flashbacks, as I regressed to being a three-year-old and recalled the abuse, I also felt the presence of Tommy and Dorothy beside me. In my mind I saw them standing there, a little boy and girl with very sad faces. They didn't say anything, but I felt comforted by them being there. They had been my soul connections during one of the darkest times of my life. Like all children I eventually let them go, but I have never forgotten them.

Who Was There for Me?

Throughout my recovery and especially during the writing of this book, I have been searching for what it was that kept my hope alive as a child. I've mentioned that music became my haven where I could escape from the world for a while. Still, I've felt that there had to have been someone that encouraged me to be who I was, while others were forcing me to be who they wanted me to be. When Tommy and Dorothy left me, I was about five years old, so I've wondered who took their place. There were many people in and out of my life as I was growing up. I thought that maybe it was one of them, but my heart told me that this special someone was a constant presence for a long time. I believe that I've finally discovered who that person was. She was my godmother, Dolores.

Aunt Dolores and Uncle Herbie were very special people in my life. We were not related to them; they were friends of my grandparents and when I was preparing to make my entrance into the world, they were asked to be my godparents. Uncle Herbie and Aunt Dolores lived in Rochester, New York, where he worked in a factory. Aunt Dolores had been a fashion model until she was diagnosed with rheumatoid arthritis in her early thirties. The disease robbed her of having a normal life. They were not able to have children of their own and they were very excited to be godparents.

Since they lived far away from us, we were only able to see them once or twice a year. I looked forward to those two weeks. In between visits, Aunt Dolores wrote me letters. Every month I received two or three and we talked on the phone often. Even when her hands became crippled and it was painful for her to write, she continued her letters to me. When we were together, Uncle Herbie and Aunt Dolores treated me with respect by allowing me to be a child, with no responsibilities except to have fun. As I look back now, it was those two weeks each year and her letters that kept my hope alive and gave me strength. She became my soul connection.

Sadly, Uncle Herbie died when he was only sixty-three from a brain aneurysm, just a few weeks before my eighteenth birthday. I was devastated that he was gone and I still needed him. I still miss his fun-loving spirit and his jokes. I wish that Duane and the kids could have known him. Then three years later, her disease defeated Aunt Dolores' life. Her body had become so fragile from all the medications that she had taken over the years to fight it. She was buried a few days later next to Uncle Herbie. The day was December 12, which happened to be Uncle Herbie's birthday.

My godparents have played such an important role in my life and have always been so special to me that when my memories started revealing the abuse, I stopped thinking about Uncle Herbie and Aunt Dolores. I was so afraid that I would learn that they were not who I thought they were, as others were revealed through my memories. I didn't want to know that they had any part in what happened to me, so I pushed them away in my heart. I was protecting myself from being hurt again. But, in my search to find the truth and to discover who had cared for me, God has revealed to my heart that my godparents were, indeed, my soul connections. There is nothing in all of the memories that I've regained that would suggest that they were not who I thought they were. My memories of them remain as precious to me as always. Once I realized this truth, my fear has gone away and my heart and mind are full of their memory. I was blessed to have such extraordinary people as my godparents. I can still feel the connection with them, even after their deaths. They continue to inspire me with hope and strength for my future.

Made in Heaven

After Uncle Herbie's death, many important things happened in my life. I turned eighteen, graduated from high school, went to work and continued to fight the control that my parents had over me. Not only was I grieving the loss of my godfather, but I felt alone and abandoned because I didn't have one of my soul connections any longer. Aunt Dolores was grieving the loss of her beloved husband and I didn't want to burden her with any of my troubles. Instead of celebrating a wonderful time in my life, I was crying myself to sleep at night because I was so lonely. Once again God brought someone into my life that would become my next and most important soul connection.

During that summer, my best friend's boyfriend became tired of me always hanging around with them. He wanted my friend Mary to himself so he figured that if he could find me someone to date, then he would have more time with her. He started telling me about a guy that he worked with, and before I knew it I had consented to go on a blind date.

The night of the date came and I was very reluctant to go. I told Mary that I had changed my mind and didn't want to go. Mary had briefly met my date before and she assured me that I would like him. "He's a nice guy," she told me. "Let's just go and have some fun, okay?" She talked me into it. We had arranged to pick up her boyfriend at work and meet my blind date at a small bar in town. On the drive there, I kept telling Mary that I changed my mind. I was very nervous. I asked again what he looked like, and they told me he had dark hair and a mustache.

The entrance was a long hallway that opened up to the bar area. We walked single file down the hall, with me being last, all the while telling Mary that I wasn't going to like him. As we entered the bar, a man with dark hair and a mustache got up and said hello to Mary's boyfriend. As he approached us, I prepared to turn and leave. He was a man in his forties and weighed about 350 pounds. Mary grabbed my arm to stop me and told me that the guy was not my date. I turned back around, the big man moved and then I saw him sitting at the bar. He stood up and introduced himself to me. His name was Duane and he had the most beautiful blue eyes I had ever seen. From that moment on, we have been inseparable. We have been through some tremendously hard times together, but our commitment to each other is strong and growing every day. When I remember that night so long ago and how close I came to walking away, I thank God for this soul connection that He has given me. There are no words that can describe the precious bond that Duane and I share, except for "made in heaven."

A Gift of Unconditional Love

Along my journey to deepening my relationship with God, I first had to develop a healthy relationship with myself. As close as Duane and I have always been, there was one thing that he could not do for me and that was to be the nurturing presence between a mother and child. God wanted me to believe in unconditional love so that I could then in turn provide that love to myself. Through a series of "coincidences" Margaret came into my life. I was so hungry for the love she gave me that I spent every moment I could with her. Since she had not been able to have children of her own, there was an awesome amount of love in her heart just waiting to be given. I was blessed to be the one to receive it. Margaret taught me to be strong and independent. She affirmed my ideas and opinions. She loved me regardless of my faults. I may have been her "Angel" but she didn't let me get away with things, either. Whenever I needed a little reminder that I wasn't perfect, I would hear her say, "Be careful sweetie, your halo is slipping."

When the time came for us to say our good-byes to each other, we cried in each other's arms. God had given each of us a wonderful gift by bringing us together and it was so hard to let it go. But, Margaret was stronger than I was. She held my hand and told me that she would never leave me. "You are truly my daughter," she said, "and nothing can keep us from being together forever. Someday we will see each other again." I have hung on to those words like a life preserver since the day she died. Because of the connection that we had in this life, I believe God will provide it again in the next. Our souls are forever intertwined. The braid that Margaret and I formed had God at the center and that braid is leading me directly to Him. Now, when I find myself reflecting on the relationship that Margaret and I had, I wonder how many other "Margaret and Loris" there are in the world, just waiting to find each other. Sometimes we have to reach out and search for what God has in store for us. When we find it, His gift to us becomes more special than all of the presents we have ever received. God's gift is truly a gift of love, given from the heart.

Sara

God's Gifts

God has provided for me a soul connection during each difficult time in my life. God knew when I needed human flesh and blood to know God's presence. These have been special people, handpicked by God so I did not have to walk the journey alone. They personified God's love and care for me. I believe my parents had a very influential part, as they were not threatened when God used people other than themselves to minister to me. They supported the soul connections God provided. This has been a wonderful and precious gift. In fact, those late nights when I sat on the stair steps beside my parents' bedroom and shared my deep inner spiritual stirrings with them, prepared me for the soul connections I would make later in life.

First Soul Connection

When I was twenty years old, my parents hosted a couple from Walter Reed Hospital for the weekend. Lou and Jane were last-minute sponsors for a group of army personnel who wanted to learn more about the Amish and Mennonites. I was fascinated with Lou's discussions and something that I cannot describe drew me to this army officer. Later I spent a weekend with my parents at Lou and Jane's home and met their daughters.

I knew Lou struggled with a severe problem of migraine headaches. When I had difficulties after my first cervical disc surgery, I experienced headaches from a myleogram test. The pain was excruciating and I knew I would find an understanding person in Lou. For the next week or more he called me every morning to connect and encourage me. He asked if he could come and visit because there was something he wanted to share with me and it could not happen over the phone.

During the visit he shared a story of his own struggle and healing. It was through his willingness to be vulnerable that I realized I needed healing of the relationship with my dad. God chose to use this unique soul connection to encourage the healing between my dad and me. This experience caused Lou and me to become more tightly braided. We remained soul connections until his death. Even now I feel closeness as I write of our shared experiences and how he touched my life.

Godly Women

Along with my mother, I have been blessed to have soul connections with two older women. Jeanne and I shared the responsibilities of deaconess at the church. Every month we visited those unable to attend church services. It was not long until we began to open our hearts to each other. She prayed for me and I prayed for her. She told me of promises from God's Word that were meaningful to her. She had a deep faith in God, which she shared with me.

Jeanne's husband was scheduled for open-heart surgery and I asked if she would like me to wait with her until the surgery was finished. She assured me that she would be fine and there was no reason for me to waste my day waiting with her. The morning of surgery I felt God impressing upon me that even though Jeanne said I should not come, it was important that I wait with her. During that time we became even more tightly braided.

Each time I return to Pennsylvania for a visit, I try to spend time with my special friend. Jeanne and I, along with her husband, share our spirits as we sit around their table having a meal or a cup of tea. Our physical connections are few and far between but the soul connection of our spirits can never be broken. We share the braid of life.

After I moved to Michigan, God connected me with another Jean. We were neighbors and attended the same church. When her husband was dying of cancer, I arranged a schedule of people from the church to help Jean with his care and to provide some meals. She was a strong, quiet woman who remained healthy, physically, spiritually and emotionally during her husband's illness.

When I was taking a correspondence course, it was required that I have a person to interact with as I studied *Celebration of Discipline* by Richard Foster. I shared with my pastor that I did not know who would be able to make a commitment of that type for me. He suggested I speak with Jean because she had been lonely since her husband died. What a wonderful gift his suggestion was for both of us. As we read, studied and shared together that oyster developed a pearl over the next three years. Not only did we find a kinship in our studies, but also in experiences.

We sat at the table; Jean with her coffee and I with my tea, sharing our souls with each other in the presence of God. We reached across the table and held hands signifying the connecting of our souls.

A Unique Blessing

Faizan is the most difficult soul connection for me to describe. He became part of my spirit even before he was born.

His mother asked if I would pray that she would be able to conceive and carry a baby full term. She and her husband had experienced several miscarriages. I began praying about their situation as God brought them to my mind. Several months later she informed me they were pregnant. Faizan was a fussy baby and a challenge for both of his parents. As he got older they asked if I would teach him English, since English was a second language for them. I spent three or four days a week with him and our souls began to knit together.

I gave him his first boots so he could walk in the snow. I watched the joy and pleasure on his face as he threw stones into the water. We laughed when he became free enough to stomp his foot in a mud puddle. I prayed for this little boy before he was born and now I had the privilege of watching him explore the world. We shared quiet moments as he snuggled up to me and we touched not only our bodies, but also our souls.

I ask myself why I feel this deep connection to a four-year-old? Through him I see much my own reaction to the spiritual world that I'm exploring. I identify with his joy of playing in the sand, kicking the leaves and causing them to rustle, and with his awe of watching the beauty of the butterflies. Just as he loves the quiet moments of being close to me, so I enjoy quiet moments with God. For me Faizan has been a reflection of my relationship with God and the spirit. Faizan and I have become braided together and share a deep love for each other.

Sara & Lori

As we have remained open to the relationships that God desires for us, we have found many people that are very precious. These connections are strong and vital to our journey of following God's will for us. Our relationships provide whatever we need, whenever we need it. We are forever grateful to God for all of the soul connections He has placed in our lives. Each person is a part of who we have become.

Pearl-descent reflections

Soul connections have happened throughout history. The story of Naomi and Ruth from the Old Testament in the book of Ruth is a wonderful example of loyalty and commitment. Both of their husbands had died, and according the culture of their day, women were seen as nothing if there wasn't a man to care for them. The futures of these two women were at stake and they were very poor. Naomi felt the need to return to her homeland of Bethlehem, hoping that her family would take care of her. Since Ruth was still young, Naomi pleaded with her to stay in her own family home where it may be easier to find a husband. Ruth loved her mother-in-law very much and did not want to lose their connection. She told Naomi that she was not willing to break their relationship. After much pleading and discussion Naomi accepted Ruth's decision to stay with her. She realized how committed Ruth was, her heart softened and she surrendered, allowing the braiding of their lives to take place.

When they arrived in Bethlehem it was the beginning of a new life for both of them. There, God provided a husband for Ruth and gifted Naomi with a grandson. They were safe, happy and cared for. God had blessed them for their commitment to each other and to Him. Ruth and Naomi's connection is unusual, but not rare. We can trust that God will bring a soul connection into our lives as well.

Another example of strong, faithful women in the Bible are Elizabeth, the mother of John the Baptist and Mary, the mother of Jesus. God had chosen these women for extraordinary missions. Elizabeth became pregnant when she was beyond the childbearing age. Mary was young, unmarried and scared when God revealed to her His plan for her life. Both of these women needed the support of each other. When Mary arrived to tell Elizabeth the news of her pregnancy, the baby leaped in Elizabeth's womb and she was filled with the Holy Spirit. Mary had sought out the person that she knew would understand and provide encouragement to her. Elizabeth was a holy woman and recognized the Spirit of God at work between them immediately and invited Mary to stay with them. Mary lived with Elizabeth for about three months until John was born. God used that time to deepen the soul connection that had occurred between the women.

God knows what is ahead for each of us. Just as God prepared Mary's body for pregnancy, He makes provisions within us for those who will become our soul connections. Our hearts and souls must remain open, ready and watchful for those that God has brought before us. He has planted the seed for a new relationship, now it is up to us to give it what it needs to grow and flourish. If we have the desire, God provides. We encourage you to go searching to find your pearls. God's promise is that they are out there, somewhere, waiting just for you.

Fuel for your journey

1. Which story caused you to think of your own experiences? Why?

2. How does it make you feel?

3. What would you like to say to God right now?

4. Who can you share these feelings with?

CHAPTER TEN

Healing
Raised to New Life

What is your image of healing? Is it peace, wholeness or is it pain and scar tissue? We've had our own questions about healing, and we shared our fear of reliving the pain in order to write our stories. As we struggled with images, a rainbow came to mind to represent the healing after the storm, but we ended our day with more questions than answers. We were not prepared for the gift we would receive from God in the morning, and this is our story of healing.

In the morning Lori began looking for the answers they had not come up with the night before. The computer was turned on and coffee was made while she struggled with her thoughts. Suddenly, she felt God urging her to go outside and sit in the swing in the backyard. It was a beautiful summer morning, with the birds singing and the sky a deep blue. There was a soft breeze blowing as she sat watching the sky. Within minutes, a wisp of clouds appeared above the trees that resembled the shape of flames. This caught Lori's attention since flames of fire will be on the cover of the book. Then she heard God's voice telling her that she would find healing in the truth. As she stared at the clouds, she thought to get her camera and take a picture of them to show Sara.

When Lori arrived back outside, the clouds had moved. As she looked up and saw them moving toward the sun, a beautiful rainbow appeared. She yelled for Sara to come outside to see this. They both knew that God had placed a message in the sky just for them. After Lori took a picture they watched as the clouds evaporated and the rainbow faded.

Hoping to see this image more clearly, they loaded the picture from the camera on to the computer. They were amazed at the picture before their eyes. From the middle cloud radiated a bright center of light. Hidden in the next cloud was an image of a cross. The rainbow formed an arch between the clouds connecting with the third one, which was wispy and transparent. In the picture they saw the Trinity. God revealed to them that as the vapors of the clouds disappeared in the radiance of the sun, so does their pain in His presence. The colors of the rainbow symbolized the diversity of each healing that they have experienced. As the colors faded away, there was nothing left between God and them. No pain, no struggles and no questions—just open hearts waiting to be filled with His Spirit. They have been healed. In the past their healings have happened on an individual basis, but now God chose them to experience complete healing together. In gratitude to God they offered their praise in a prayer of faith.

Sara

My Healing

I had shared with Lori that I did not want to write about healing. How could I write about a subject that brought me so many questions and guilt? For thirty years I've wondered if I would have been healed if I had obeyed the woman who had told me I would be healed if I removed my neck brace. Was my faith too weak to experience a miracle?

After seeing the cloud formation and the rainbow, we were in total awe and entered our own world with God as we listened to praise music. It was then God revealed to me that I had experienced healing through the doctors. God could have healed me through a miracle that day, but God had other plans. God trusted me enough to share love and develop a relationship with the neurosurgeon and his family. This was God's plan and I did not settle for second best. What a freeing revelation, and my questions evaporated in the presence of God. My questions were not wrong, for God could handle each of them. It was that in the presence of God the questions were no longer important.

Through the relationship built with the surgeon and his family, we remained in close contact for more than five years. We celebrated the birth of their children and attended birthday parties. His wife thought of me as one of her close friends and it was to me that she turned in times of trouble. This provided me the opportunity to share with her God's love. I was faithful to the trust God had placed in me. The healing I experienced as I looked at the clouds and rainbow has replaced the guilt with peace and contentment.

Peace in the Storm

Peace is a by-product of healing. Peace comes to us by many paths. Sue was a patient I met in the hospital as I was making chaplain visits. She was in her eighties, lived alone and had fallen in her bedroom. She had enjoyed good health until this incident occurred. Her two children lived at a distance, so their visits were infrequent. After many tests, it was decided that she needed open-heart surgery. She did not recover as was expected and remained on a ventilator for several weeks.

I visited with her almost every day to hold her hand and encourage her. Sometimes I would acknowledge that she was going through a difficult struggle but she was never alone because God was with her. When she began improving, Sue was given a writing board so she could communicate. She wrote that she had so much to tell me. After the ventilator was removed, she told me she had experienced God. She reached for my hand and I asked her if everything was okay. She nodded and smiled, squeezing my hand.

Sue continues to experience heart failure, but she is at peace. She sold her home and moved to a health care facility close to her children. When we talk on the phone I hear a woman who knows healing of the spirit even though her body continues to deteriorate. She is living in peace and contentment.

Dark Night of the Soul

How do we deal with the times we have asked God for healing and nothing happens? During an extended time of illness I had been to many doctors and they were unable to discern why the particular symptoms were present. I felt I should ask the elders and pastor of the church to anoint me, believing God would bring healing. I invited my friends to be part of the experience with me. I believed God could heal me, but my symptoms continued. Did God not hear our prayers? Was there not enough faith present among the group? Was I not worthy of God's healing touch? These were questions that plagued my mind.

During this "dark night of the soul" I needed friends to pray and support me because not only was my body weak and weary, but also my soul was dried up. Even in the midst of the dryness God was present and I saw God in the kindness exhibited by precious friends. They brought our family meals, drove me to the doctors, prayed daily for me and sat in solidarity with me. It is in times of darkness that we see the light of God most clearly. This is when we cling to the light as one about to die. Our knowledge and experience of God grows deeper as we seek God's face and presence in our particular situation. When the dark night ends, we will reflect upon our loneliness and dryness as a meaningful time of inner growth.

Loss and Healing

I had the opportunity to observe a different type of healing as I sat with an elderly couple as they discussed the report from the doctor. They had been told the husband would die within twenty-four hours if he chose not to have dialysis. The wife sat by the bedside holding the hand of her husband as they talked about what was the best decision for them. They cried and held each other close as they came to the conclusion to spend the next twenty-four hours together waiting for him to be relieved of his pain. The family gathered and they said their good-byes and shared memories. Although there was sadness and grief in their choice, healing and peace were part of this family's experience.

Gradual Healing

Because the power of shame had been a stronghold in my life, my healing experience in relation to shame has been a process. Initially I was not able to recognize my "illness" or give it a name. As the truth of my "disease" became revealed to me I had the option of dealing with it or ignoring the truth. I chose to face my disease and allow myself to feel the pain and agony shame had caused my spirit. The healing came one step at a time as I accepted the truth and allowed my spirit to remain open for the Great Physician to do the surgery. The Physician's hands were loving and gentle, but the surgery was painful even though I knew healing would ultimately come to my spirit. I did not go through the surgery alone. Because no anesthetic was used the Physician had the team available to comfort and support me with their presence during the surgery. I was wide awake and very aware of everything that happened. It was of utmost importance that the healthcare team embraced me. Surgery was exhausting, but recovery brought hope to my spirit as each day I felt stronger.

Each healing experience I've had has raised me to new life. It has brought a deeper meaning to my existence. Sometimes the healings have been small and more ordinary, like noticing a lowness of spirit. I find at those times I need to find a place of healing. It may be listening to a favorite CD, going for a walk, reading Scripture, sitting in a favorite chair and listening to God, or giving myself permission to cry as the tears cleanse my soul. When we lived in Pennsylvania and were closer to the ocean I told Les several times that I would be fine if I could spend several hours alone on the beach listening to the rhythmic breaking of the waves. The wind has also been healing for me as I visualize the Holy Spirit as the wind blowing upon me bringing to me freshness and renewal. God has as many ways to bring healing as the varied hues of a rainbow, each color bringing to us God's love and a message of hope, peace and newness of life.

Lori
Where Were You?

During our trip to REM in Chicago, Sara and I felt that we had been welcomed into a world of love, compassion and spirituality. I have never been comfortable attending seminars and meeting new people. But this time was different. These were unique people that followed the movements of the Holy Spirit in their lives closely. Also, I have become more comfortable in my relationship with God and where He is leading me. We believe that this trip was predestined for Sara and me. God wanted us there for a particular reason and we obeyed.

Everywhere we went we made new connections and friends. The people attending were from every area of the country and of many different faiths. But we all had one thing in common, our love for helping others. The rooms were filled with chaplains and C.P.E. students. We learned together and joined in worship with different cultures. The conception of our book took place at REM, so Sara and I enjoyed working together with Urias on the area that God wanted us to focus on. Each day was special, but the ending of the conference was a sacred event for us.

As we joined in the closing worship service, we were energized by the message given by the minister. She spoke of what we can learn from strong women in the Bible. The most important thing we learned is that once you start moving forward toward Jesus, you can never go back. No matter how bad things get, or how tired we become and in spite of what life throws at us, we have to keep moving forward. Her message inspired me and at times I felt that she was talking directly to me.

At the closing of the sermon, she invited all who wished to have the elders in the congregation lay hands on us in prayer to come forward. Sara and I held hands and walked to the stage together. There were many people, all going in the same direction, but we held tightly to each other so we wouldn't be separated. We steadily made our way to the minister who had just given us the message to not turn back. It was as if our feet knew exactly where to take us. We recognized God's spirit and we followed. As we stood in front of her for our blessing, she put her arms around both of us at the same time. She prayed that we would always follow the Spirit. When she released us, Sara and I were both shaking. Next, we went to another person we had admired as a strong woman in the group. She anointed Sara's forehead with oil, held her and prayed for her. I stood there shaking with the excitement of the Spirit and moved forward for my anointing. She held me and rocked me, asking Jesus to take care of me. She prayed for the Spirit to give me strength and for God to provide the answers that I was searching for.

As she released me I felt my knees buckle and I sat down on the floor. Sara was also visibly touched by this experience and we just held each other. Suddenly I knew that a flashback was beginning. My hands were shaking and I was crying. I looked up and Whit was there. He had seen what was happening and came quickly to be at our sides. He asked me what I needed. I kept repeating loudly that I needed Urias, right now. Urias was there, but he was playing the piano and didn't realize what had happened. By now, there were several people surrounding me, praying for me, people that I didn't know and some that I did. Someone heard me yell for Urias and they went to get him.

In my flashback, I was once again three years old and hiding under my little brother's crib. I was rocking back and forth and crying. I kept yelling, "Where is he? I need him." When Urias made his way to me, he immediately sat on the floor and held me, telling me that he was there. I looked at him and said, "Where were you? I've been yelling for you." He assured me that he was there now and I was okay. No one was ever going to hurt me again. As he rocked me, I suddenly felt peaceful and safe. In my mind, as I sat there under the crib, it was God's arms around me, rocking me. It was God that I had been yelling for and He let me know through Urias that He had been there with me right from the beginning. I was never alone. I didn't have to be afraid any longer.

Urias held me for a long time, constantly reminding me that I was safe. When I finally stopped shaking and crying, I told him what I had remembered. Together we praised God. I had never felt more peaceful in my entire life. Sara, Whit, Urias and I sat there for a long time talking about what had happened. There had been one particular woman that was next to me praying when my flashback began. Her touch and words were so comforting to me. Before we left this moment, we all had our picture taken together. We sat in a huddle with our arms around each other, black hands holding white. It's a very beautiful picture that represents the wonderful experience of REM for Sara and me.

Later as we were driving home, we were reflecting on all that had happened to us in such a short period of time. I thought about the flashback and how it was different than all the others. Suddenly, the message that God had given me in those moments came to me very clearly. I turned to Sara and said, "I've just had my last flashback. I'm never going to have another one." That's what God was trying to tell me. There is no reason to be afraid of my past, because I am certain that He was there taking care of me. Right then, I knew in my heart that my flashback experiences were over.

In the months since REM, God has been true to His promise. I have had many memories return and while they are painful, I have not had to experience them though another flashback. Now, instead of the shaking that had preceded a memory, I become very anxious with many thoughts going through my mind, until at last I focus on just one. Then it slowly returns. The most difficult part is actually verbalizing what I'm remembering. Sometimes it just seems too horrible for words, but once I'm able to say it, I can move past it.

REM has become a dear memory of hope for me. Our vision of the book was born there and my fear that God didn't care what was happening to me as a child has been healed. This hope and my faith in Him has indeed changed my life. I now have the courage to move forward, always following the Spirit.

The Scars of a Miracle

There are many different ways of emotional healing and they can be as painful as wounds to your body after an accident. The pain that I felt inside after I began remembering what was done to me was excruciating and hard to describe to anyone that had not experienced something similar. It was very hard to find an image of my pain so that others could understand. Unfortunately, my son knows. He has felt the same intense pain, but his was of the physical kind.

A few months after my first memories returned, I was in therapy and had developed several soul connections with people in the pastoral care department of the hospital. These relationships became my lifelines of strength and were essential to my survival after we received the most horrible phone call that a parent can receive; Jason had been in a car accident.

Jase and three of his friends had gone to Florida for spring break. It was his first trip there and he loved it. They had a wonderful time and were on the way home when a drunk driver slammed into the back of their van. The force of the impact caused Jason's vehicle to crash into the guardrail and he was thrown out onto the highway. After rolling several times on the pavement, he came to a stop. As he looked up, cars were coming toward him. Amazingly, he had enough strength to get off the road. He was rushed to the hospital before we even knew of the accident.

When we arrived, we were so grateful that he was alive that we didn't realize the extent of his injuries. He had suffered road rash over most of his body. The skin on his back had been ripped off as he slid down the road. There was a deep gash in his scalp that had taken several staples to close. The doctors explained that he also had skull and jaw fractures. Everyone at the hospital was amazed that he had survived and hadn't sustained any further internal injuries.

The pain was excruciating and he was given strong medication to help relieve it. Bandages and ointment needed to be applied every few hours, which caused more pain. Taking a shower was torture since the touch of the water hitting the raw skin on his back sent ripples of agony through him.

I watched as Jase struggled to regain his strength. His will and determination were strong and they helped him to survive the weeks and months of healing. It wasn't long before I realized that the wounds that Jason had received were very much like the wounds that I was carrying on my soul. This inspired me to face my pain by following the example of courage that my son was setting for me. He didn't let the pain take over. He fought it and won. We knew that it was hard for him to allow us to help him do the littlest things, but he did. Jason understood that he could not heal on his own, he needed help from those who love him.

This was a lesson that I learned from him. My healing is happening because I surrendered and allowed God and my soul connections to nurse my wounds. Jase and I are each left with scars that will always be with us. They have become a part of who we are. After Jason's accident, whenever I saw his scars, I became angry because my son's perfect body had been forever changed. But, then one day the anger faded as I realized that the scars would always remind me that Jason survived when he should not have. So did I. I can say that I have survived and have been healed. Our scars will always give testimony to the power of God's love.

This is one of the truths that God told me on the morning the clouds and rainbow appeared. Before I was aware of the truth hidden deep inside of me, I was not free. This secret controlled me for more than forty years. It had an effect on my entire life. The revelation of my hidden memories has allowed the secret to be told, and in the process I have been freed. My wounds are healing because of God's touch. Just as the clouds evaporated and created the beautiful colors in the rainbow, my pain has dissipated into a rainbow of strength, peace, joy and healing.

Healing Reflections

In John 5:1-15 we read the story of a man who had been an invalid for thirty-eight years. He was sitting beside a pool near one of the gates in Jerusalem.

As Jesus approached the man, He asked, "Do you want to get well?"

"Who is this man coming to me and asking if I want to get well?" he thought to himself. "I have nobody to help me into the pool," he responded. "So how can I be healed? Every day I have come for thirty-eight years, but someone else gets in before I can wiggle myself into the water."

Then the stranger said, "Stand up. Pick up your mat and walk."

The man could not believe what he was hearing, but he obeyed. He felt strength and energy surge through his once limp useless body. He stood up and walked away.

But that was not the end of the story. Some religious people were watching this event. "What are you doing carrying your mat on the Sabbath?" they questioned him.

"The man who healed me told me to pick up my mat and walk," he replied.

They fired back at him with another question. "Who was this man who told you to pick up your mat and walk?"

He looked around in bewilderment. "I don't know he didn't tell me his name and I didn't ask. All I know is that it is great to be able to walk. I no longer need to live by the pool. My life is forever changed."

Later Jesus found the man and identified Himself and shared with him some words of wisdom. The healed man found those who had questioned him and reported to them that a man named Jesus had healed him.

How does this story relate to our experiences of healing? Like the man at the pool we have varied reasons why we are dealing with the situation that is confronting us. Perhaps we enjoy the attention and concern. Or our problem relieves us of a responsibility that we fear. Maybe it is the way we were raised, our choice of a spouse or lack of a spouse, the difficulties and pain wayward children have brought into our life. On the other hand we may have become so accustomed to our circumstances that it has become a way of life for us. Jesus is aware of our condition and confronts us with the question, "Do you want to be healed?"

When healing comes, others may not understand it. The validity of the process or timing may be questioned. In fact the source of the healing may be debated. After Jesus identified Himself, the healed man did not fear letting others know who healed him. The power and presence of God is the ultimate healer in our lives and for that we give God the glory.

Numbers 6:24-26 offers a prayer of blessing and healing used by the Jewish priests,

> *"The Lord bless you and keep you; the Lord*
> *make his face shine upon you and be gracious to*
> *you; the Lord turn his face toward you and give*
> *you peace."*

This is our prayer for your journey,

> *That you will see God's face shining upon you*
> *and know the peace that only God can bring.*
> *Some say that the appearance of a rainbow*

*symbolizes God smiling with love for His chil-
dren. May you always search for the rainbow at
the end of your storm and feel God's love as He
pours His Mercy on you.*

Fuel for your journey

1. Which story caused you to think of your own experiences? Why?

2. How does it make you feel?

3. What would you like to say to God right now?

4. Who can you share these feelings with?

CHAPTER ELEVEN

Celebration

Dancing with God

Why do we celebrate? Do we celebrate alone or with others? Is celebration important? How do we celebrate?

Elsa answered the phone a bit annoyed with the interruption. Suddenly her mind clicked into gear as she recognized her sister's voice.

"I'm a grandma! Amy had a baby girl and they're both fine. I've delivered so many babies as a midwife, but it was the most awesome experience to be able to deliver my own first grandchild." She took a breath to regain her composure.

"Judy, I'm so happy for you. There's nothing like being a grandma! I can't even imagine what it must have been like to help with the birth of the baby. What did she weigh and do they have a name chosen?" Elsa had caught her sister's joy.

Judy laughed and replied, "They named her Elizabeth Jo and she weighed 5 pounds 6 ounces. She's the most beautiful baby ever—of course I'm grandma, but she is gorgeous. Joe shook his head when I told him I was going out to buy Elizabeth some cute little girl clothes."

"You really have caught the excitement of being a grandma." Elsa smiled.

"You're right, there's nothing like it." Judy's voice was heavy with emotion. The "hat" of a midwife had been left in the office. "Do you think maybe you could come to the hospital and see her tonight? It would be great if you could."

"Of course, I'll come and see my sister's first grandchild. I'll meet you at seven."

Happy events are to be shared with others. Celebration requires that community join with us. A party is not a party unless others are invited. The dance of celebration has begun. All heaviness and despair is left at the door and we are invited to join the party of God's children. God approaches and asks, "May I have this dance?"

The dance symbolizes our relationship with God. He leads us in the right steps, but sometimes He lets us try to lead on our own. He doesn't mind when we slip and step on His toes. When we go too far and get out of step, He gently takes the lead again and holds us close while we learn. There are times when He sits back and lets us dance for Him. In His presence, we feel graceful and beautiful, even when we make a mistake. We feel His encouragement and pride in us as we learn the new steps.

Lori

Fixing My Voice

At night, when I'm sleeping, my spirit continues to struggle with the issues that have recently surfaced in my life. For several weeks, my dreams have been nightmares as I have fought to claim my voice. My mind has created wars going on or someone chasing me. In order to survive, I find places to hide and be very quiet. Eventually, I am found and I try to scream, but nothing comes out. I wake up exhausted and scared. I believe that this has been a battle between my inner child and myself. I want to use my voice to tell others about God's truths, but the little girl within me has been fighting to keep me quiet. She knows that in our past when we tried to tell the truth of what was happening, we were punished. The little girl is trying to protect herself.

Things are changing between us, though. We are becoming stronger together and she has learned to trust again. My voice is stronger and more confident. Yet, the dreams have continued. Then I realized that the little girl in me had never been given the chance to use her voice, to tell what happened in her own words. Recently, as another memory was coming back, I sat down with a piece of paper and pencil and began to write my thoughts. I was remembering the incident as a child, so I allowed myself to write as a child. When I was done, the memory faded and I was peaceful. Later, as I read what I had written I was amazed at the pain that my little girl was able to release. She talked about her baby brother and her favorite doll. The fear was there as her mommy and daddy were fighting. The sadness was powerful as she wrote about telling her mommy what was happening to her and not being believed. My little girl decided that it was better not to talk about it, so she "lost" her voice.

I cried and rejoiced at the same time. I had given her back her voice. My journey of pain and healing has brought me to a place of celebration. In honor of the progress I have made, I decided to try to find the doll that was my favorite and missed so badly. My doll had been "sent to a doll hospital" by my parents when I was little and she didn't come back. I never forgot her, though, so I went online to Ebay, to find another one like her. It wasn't too difficult to find a Chatty Cathy doll made in 1960 that I could afford. Unfortunately, her voice does not work when I pull the string, just like my first doll. She was sent away because her voice was broken. My voice was broken, also. God has fixed mine and I will fix hers. Now, I have my doll back again. She sits with me as I write. I feel a sense of completeness whenever I look at her. I think I'll buy her a new dress for our celebration party.

Instead of the nightmares that I was having, I now dream of speaking to groups of people and sharing my stories. In one particular dream, I had arranged for Urias to speak at a meeting. There were many people sitting at conference tables. When we were ready to begin, Urias asked me to say an opening prayer. I started to speak, but my voice was soft and low. Urias interrupted me by saying, "Speak loud and clear, my dear, so that everyone will hear you." I prayed a prayer of thanks to God. When I looked up, the meeting had changed into a party. People were receiving gifts that they had waited a long time for. Everyone was so happy.

As I reflected on my dream the next morning it became clear to me that I had found my voice. The presents that people were receiving were the gifts of God's truths as I shared them in my prayer. The battles are over. God has won. I am now able to go out and use my voice with a wholeness of my mind, body and spirit. What a celebration!

Celebration vs. Grief

Shortly after I began my C.P.E. internship at the hospital, I was privileged to be present with a family as they struggled between celebration and grief. A young couple that was expecting their first child requested a visit from the chaplain. The mother had been admitted due to premature labor. When I answered the page, the nurse explained that the situation was very sad. The baby had several things wrong and would not live outside of the mother's womb.

As I stood outside the door of the patient's room, my heart was heavy with sadness for this family. I was also feeling afraid of not being experienced enough to provide the care that they deserved. My soul was pleading for God to take me out of the situation, but He didn't. There was no one else available. This was up to me. I took a deep breath, prayed for God's guidance and walked inside.

I introduced myself to the parents. They were in their mid-twenties, but they looked like kids to me. Julie was sitting on the bed with her husband, Jim, next to her. He had his right arm around her shoulders and his other hand resting gently on her tummy, feeling the baby move. Julie and Jim explained to me that they had known for several weeks that the baby had severe problems. When the diagnosis was made that the baby would not survive once it was born, the doctors recommended that they terminate the pregnancy. They had prayed and discussed it together. Julie and Jim knew that as long as the baby was in the womb, it was still alive. Their decision was to continue with the pregnancy for as long as they could. They wanted the baby to feel their love and presence. Those few precious months gave them the time to give their baby a lifetime of love. They sang to it, read stories and talked to the baby constantly. Because of the abnormalities the baby had, it wasn't possible for the doctors to know if it was a boy or girl, but it didn't matter to Julie and Jim. The nickname they had chosen fit for either, so they spoke of the baby by name.

My fear of not knowing how to help them disappeared as I listened to their story. God had already helped them. I deeply admired their strength and courage. They had accepted that this baby would only be with them for a short time and they celebrated the time they had. I thanked God for placing me in this situation, with people of such deep faith. I wondered what my role as chaplain would be for this couple.

Within moments, that role became clear. Jim explained that they had planned that their minister from church would be present at the birth in order to baptize the baby immediately. Unfortunately, Julie had gone into labor early and the minister was out of town. They asked if I would be available to go to the delivery room with them and baptize their baby. At this time in my training I had never baptized a baby and had definitely not been present at a birth. Every cell in my body was scared and shaking, but I said yes. I felt honored to be asked to be a part of this sacred time.

The next thing I knew I was putting on scrubs, gown and a mask. I followed Jim as Julie was wheeled into the delivery room. It was decided that a caesarean section would give the baby the best chance of living for a few minutes after birth. Julie was prepped for surgery, but remained awake. I took my place with Jim at her side. We prayed together and then the surgery began. Within moments the baby was delivered. The nurse gently placed the baby in the warming table. She motioned for me to come quickly.

I picked up the holy water and oil and went to the baby. When I saw it, I choked back a sob. The baby was so badly deformed that I couldn't tell if it was a boy or girl. I looked at the nurse, who was softly crying also, and asked. She told me it was a girl and she was barely alive. I focused my eyes on the baby's face. She was so beautiful, with tiny features. Her arms and legs were also perfect. The deformities were on her torso. All of the internal organs had grown on the outside of her little body.

Julie and Jim had given me the names they had chosen for the baby. Quickly, I blessed the baby with oil. My hands were shaking as I made the sign of the cross on her forehead. Next, I gently poured the holy water on her head, baptizing her in the name of the Father, the Son and the Holy Spirit. I asked for God's blessing on His child, Angela Kaylene, which means, "angel sent from heaven." When the baptism was finished, I stood there for a moment looking at this beautiful little girl and I asked God, "Why?" I tenderly touched her cheek, said hello and good-bye to her and went back to her parents.

When I reached them, I held their hands and told them they had a little girl. They began to cry as I told them how beautiful she was and that she had been baptized. As the doctors continued to close Julie's incision, I prayed a blessing for Angela's parents. After the prayer, Jim asked me if I would go and tell their family members that were waiting that they had a daughter.

God had not answered my "why" question, so I was a little angry as I left the delivery room. I ripped the mask and gown off. It wasn't fair. How can God let an innocent little baby like that suffer so much? I knew that I wouldn't get the answer I was looking for and I needed to go to the family, so I put my anger on hold.

The family was in the waiting room and as I walked down the hall I saw that the room was full. There were about thirty people, some talking, others on phones and several sitting quietly. A hush fell over the room as I entered. Two women approached me immediately, introducing themselves as Julie and Jim's moms. Everyone else stood up when I said that I was the chaplain. I explained that I had been able to baptize the baby, and that Jim and Julie were doing okay.

"Is the baby still alive?" one mom asked. I nodded.

"Is it a boy or girl?" the other mom said.

Tears came to my eyes as I softly said, "It's a girl. Angela Kaylene."

Both women hugged me, thanking me for being there to baptize their granddaughter. Everyone in the room was hugging each other, laughing and crying at the same time. I stood there in the middle of their celebration and their grief. I had never seen anything like it before or since. Angela had grandparents, aunts and uncles, cousins and friends that loved her, celebrating her birth and in moments would grieve her death.

The next day I went to see Julie and Jim. She was getting ready to go home. I thanked them for allowing me to be part of Angela's life. They were very grateful that I had been there to baptize her. There were several pictures that they shared with me of the baby. The nurses had put together a remembrance package together which included the baby's foot and hand prints, pictures, baptismal certificate, etc. This was all they had to take home with them. But, they had many memories of the time that they had spent with her before her birth. There was also time to hold her. Angela had died peacefully in her parents' arms within an hour.

During the most painful moments of my life, when I think that it's impossible to find anything to celebrate, I think of Angela and her family. They are my inspiration to look for the good in the bad. God has still not explained to me why this baby died, but I have accepted that it is part of the mystery of life and death. Yet, even in her suffering, Angela became the motivation for an immense amount of love, strength and faith. This little girl will always be a part of my heart, a tiny angel from heaven.

Donkey in the Well

Life is filled with celebration. We need only to stop for a moment, look around and listen. The birds chattering in the trees, the crickets singing their song, the gentle breeze that falls across your face and the warmth of the sunshine peeking through the window that calls to you to wake up. It's a new day. A day that is full of promise, new beginnings and adventures waiting to happen. Celebrate!

But, sometimes the day doesn't feel like a day of celebration because of the pain and struggle that it brings. Maybe your days are filled with endless chores, financial problems, depression and illness. What do you do? Most celebrations do not come to us easily, but rather through long hard work, frustrations and tears. Persistence and perseverance will bring about the sweetest celebrations in our lives. We look forward to when we can finally feel the joy, when all of our suffering is done.

Once upon a time, on an afternoon a very long time ago, a donkey was walking across the field. It had been a very hard day of pulling the heavy plow for the farmer that owned her. The sun was setting low over the trees as she slowly made her way back to her home in the barn to eat hay and drink water. Every muscle in her body ached as she walked, but she kept on, knowing that soon she would rest.

Just ahead she saw the barn and the farmer filling her trough with food. She was almost there, when suddenly the ground beneath her collapsed and she fell. The donkey kept falling down, further and further into the dark. At last, she stopped falling. When she looked up, she could see a little bit of light near the top. She tried to jump and climb up, but it was impossible. The donkey was very scared, lonely and tired. She lay down on the ground, with her eyes looking up and wondered how she would ever get out of there.

Early the next morning, the farmer went to the barn to begin his chores. When he came to the donkey's pen, he noticed that the food and water had not been touched. Then he realized that she wasn't there. He searched frantically for her, but she was nowhere to be found. He wondered if she ever came in from the field the night before. Quickly, he finished feeding the rest of the animals and set out to find his donkey.

The day wore on and the sun became hot. The farmer was ready to give up. As he tiredly walked back toward the barn, he thought he heard a noise. It sounded close, but he didn't see anything. He walked a little further and heard it again. The sound was coming from an old dried-up well nearby. He ran to the well, looked down and saw the donkey. She was hot, dirty, hungry and thirsty, but otherwise okay. The farmer sat down on the ground next to the well and wondered how he would get her out. She was too heavy for him to pull out with a rope, he didn't have any equipment to use and if he couldn't get her out, she would starve to death. He laid his head in his hands. It was useless. He felt totally helpless. The only thing to do would be to fill the well with dirt. The donkey would not suffer as long as she would without food or water. He did not want to lose his best donkey, but he had no choice. Sadly, he walked to the barn to get a shovel.

When the farmer told his friends and family what he needed to do, they offered to help him in order to get the job done quickly. They gathered at the well. The farmer prayed for God to give them strength and they began shoveling dirt into the well.

The donkey looked up at the dirt falling on top of her. She didn't like the heaviness of it on her back, so she shook it off. But, more dirt came down the well and landed on her. She didn't understand what was happening, but she knew that she did not like it. Once again, she shook her body until the dirt fell off. The donkey continued to shake as the dirt fell. Eventually, the ground below her began to fill with the loose dirt. There was no place for her to go, but up. She stepped up and realized that it brought her a little closer to the opening of the well. The donkey became very excited, so she kept shaking each time a shovel full of dirt fell into the well.

When the well was about half filled, the farmer looked in to see that she had been buried and was no longer suffering. His mouth dropped open when he saw the donkey looking back at him. He shouted for joy that she was still alive and making her way to the top by stepping up onto the dirt. Everyone was amazed and began to shovel the dirt faster and faster. The donkey did her part by shaking it off and stepping up. Before long she was near the top of the well. Then she was there. Close enough to jump out on her own. The farmer ran to her and hugged her around her neck. The donkey was filled with new energy and so grateful to be free that she danced around that well. The farmer and his friends celebrated with a feast of food and wine, while the donkey ate and drank her fill back in her home in the barn.

This was a story that I had heard several years ago and it has always stayed with me as an example of courage and determination. Circumstances in my life have helped me to relate to the donkey. The well in my life became a pit of despair as the dirt was heaped upon me. With every shovel full of abuse, control, shame and fear came the possibility of being buried alive. The heaviness of it threatened to pull me down. But, as I was able to really look at the dirt, I realized that I did not own it. God showed me how to let it go and shake it off. As I did, I learned how to stand up for myself and step up. The process was long and slow. I struggled along the way, but I kept my focus on the top of the well. Now, I'm close enough to jump out and be free. The celebration that God had waiting for me is sweet and precious. I am sharing my feast of the fruit harvested from the gifts of the Holy Spirit by telling my story. This is a celebration that will not end. In fact, it is only the beginning.

Sara

May I Have This Dance?

It had been a heavy day of tedious class interaction and hospital visitations ladened with sadness. I was on call that night and found solitude in the sleep room. I lay exhausted on the bed reviewing the day. Not only was my body weary, but also my inner being was crying out for peace, continuity and rest.

I closed my eyes seeking refuge with God. It was then that I felt God asking me to dance. "Sara, take hold of my hand and join me on the dance floor."

"I'm too tired," I replied with fatigue. "It has been a rough day and I need to rest."

"Come to me and I will give you rest," was the offer.

I contemplated God's proposal and slowly stretched out my hand. God wrapped my body in arms of love and compassion. With gentleness I was guided to join the dance. No words were needed as I leaned into God's embrace. The exhaustion evaporated as I surrendered myself and joined the celebration.

Celebration may be the activity farthest from our minds in the midst of the pressures of life. The energy has been drained out of us and our spirits are heavy. God's invitation brings forth a sigh and we wonder if God is sane to think we have enough energy to celebrate.

These are the situations when I try to remember to place my trust in God's wisdom, rather than my own feelings. God is offering me a gift and all that is being asked of me is to accept the offer. It is then that I can celebrate God's presence in my life.

"A Celebration Oops"

Sometimes our celebrations are not as glorious as we anticipated. I remember as a child on the farm there was much garden work that needed to be done. Our parents told us that if we worked hard we could get the necessary chores completed and spend the Fourth of July at a state park. We pulled together as a team, energized with the thought of spending the day at the park, swimming. When we arrived, the picnic tables among the trees were taken so we were forced to eat our lunch in the sweltering sun. The lake had little more to offer as everybody stood in the water with limited opportunity to swim. We were disappointed that our hope of celebration fell short of our expectations. We laughed and said, " Never again would we plan to go to the park on a holiday."

In the celebrations we plan, disappointment and disillusionment are sometimes the result. Our expectations are high and the outcome is less than what we had hoped. God-ordained events never leave us empty. Rather our empty heart is filled with joy and gratitude that we were invited to the party. As a result our strength is renewed and we bring to life new hope and trust in a God who desires the best for us.

Join the Party

Because I've grown up with a strong work ethic, it is difficult for me to celebrate just because I'm invited to a party. Celebrations carry a strong mandate of reward. I can only party after the work has been completed. God has placed fun-loving friends in my path who have helped me to loosen up and celebrate. I'm learning to view life as an adventure and find moments of fun along the way.

I was busy studying and our friends called asking us to come over for a cookout.

I replied, "I have so much to do. I really don't have the time."

"You need a break and it will do you good just to get away from the books," he reasoned.

"Well, it can't be late," I responded. "I need to get up early tomorrow morning."

"Great, we'll see you in about half an hour."

When we arrived we were told the evening was perfect for a boat ride before we ate. We glided through the canal into the open waters. The boat responded to the acceleration of the throttle. I climbed to the bow and thrilled as the wind whipped through my hair. I felt my energy and creativity being renewed. I relaxed as I let the responsibilities of the day be chased away. The cookout was the culmination of the evening.

The studies were not completed; the work was still before me. I had experienced the joy of celebration, and a good night's sleep provided the refreshment I needed to begin a new day.

New Life

Working as a chaplain on the cardiac floor provided an opportunity to walk with others through their time of celebration. Dan was a forty-two-year-old man who had been scheduled for a heart catheterization. The results required immediate attention. His wife sat beside his bed, her face etched with worry.

After initial greetings the wife said, "This is such a shock. He didn't pass his stress test so they scheduled this heart cath and now they tell us they are going to do open heart surgery tomorrow."

"It is almost more than you can process," I reflected.

"He's hardly been sick a day in his life. I guess we'll get through this somehow," she added.

"I realize this is a shock, but you will get through it one day at a time. Is there anything more I can do for you this evening? I'll be stopping by tomorrow morning before surgery."

The next morning I explained how the chaplains would update the family during the surgery. They asked that I say a prayer. During the day I watched the anxiety be replaced with relief as the family was able to see their husband and father in the recovery room.

Several days later I visited Dan. He was resting and hoping to go home the next day.

"I want to thank you for being there for my family," he said. "It was a hard time for them."

I replied, "I was glad to provide support and care during your surgery."

His eyes became misty as he began. "I feel as though I have a new lease on life. This was a wake-up call for me. I'm a changed man." I noticed a smile cross his face as his wife entered the room.

"Chaplain, I'm so glad you are here. Thank you so much for your prayers and support. I don't know what we would have done without you." She reached for her husband's hand.

I smiled and rejoiced in their celebration of new life.

Dancing Reflections

The story of Hagar, Sarah and Abraham is one of intrigue. It had been twenty-four years since God promised Sarah's husband, Abraham, that he would have a son through whom a nation would be born. Those years were tedious as each month Sarah was unable to become pregnant. Every year only added to her disappointment and feeling of failure. Her only desire was to be able to give her husband a son. Why was God not keeping the promise?

Sarah, after waiting so many years, unfolded a brilliant idea. One evening she approached Abraham. "God has promised you on several occasions that you would become a father of many nations. I am getting older and fear I will soon be unable to have a child. Sleep with Hagar, my slave-girl, and by that means you will have a son."

Hagar, the Egyptian slave-girl, had no voice in the decision. Abraham slept with her and she became pregnant. Sarah became jealous of Hagar's pregnancy and abused the voiceless slave-girl. Sarah's abuse became so great that Hagar chose to run away.

Her bondage was oppressive and she sought refuge in the wilderness. It was there that Hagar received a message from the

Lord. She was asked where she had come from and where she was going. Hagar was told to return to Sarah and submit to her. Then she was promised that her offspring would become more than could be numbered. In Hagar's desperate situation God spoke.

The circumstances did not change, but God communicated with Hagar. She returned to her mistress and together they anticipated the birth of a son, who was named Ishmael, meaning "God hears." Ishmael brought much joy to this previously childless family. They found contentment knowing that this child would fulfill God's promise to Abraham.

A new twist to the story is revealed when Sarah overheard some visitors talking with her husband. One of them said, "About this time next year your wife, Sarah, will have a son." Sarah could not believe what she heard and laughed in amusement thinking that she in her old age would give birth to a child.

Soon Sarah's womb was carrying a new life and her spirit was pregnant with joy and purpose. Within a year, Isaac was born to Sarah and Abraham. Sarah no longer needed Ishmael to fulfill God's promise. She told Abraham he must send Hagar and her son away.

Again, Hagar found herself at the mercy of others, she was a voiceless object to be discarded when no longer of any use. Abraham gave Hagar some bread and water and told her that she and Ishmael had to leave. Hagar was in the desert and her son was about to die. She wept for him and gave her agony a voice. God heard and told her not to be afraid. God would make a great nation of her son. It was then that she saw a well of water and was able to give Ishmael a drink. They lived in the wilderness and later Hagar found her son an Egyptian wife.

Celebration is revealed in this story of God's grace given to both Hagar and Sarah. In Sarah, we see the privileged calling out to God and making wrong choices in attempting to help God. But, the God of grace was faithful and provided the son of promise for Sarah. How often do we settle for substitutes in our lives? We search for fulfillment and purpose in vocations, food, marriage and children. Like Sarah we attempt to help God with the plans. Our scheming only brings more problems that need to be tackled.

Hagar's troubles continued to increase and we search for a God of grace and mercy. In the midst of oppression could Hagar celebrate? Hagar's celebration was maybe the most profound, in that it was an intimate dance, just between her and God. She was recognized as a person of worth and value. The promise was given that God would make a great nation of her descendants. Although God heard her voice, the circumstances of life did not change. Through these situations, Hagar found her voice and we celebrate with her.

At various times of life we, like Sarah, enjoy the powerful position of privilege. We make our own choices and then discover a God who rescues us from our troubles. On the other hand, there are times we feel like Hagar and experience the oppression of others. Regardless of our efforts, situations move from bad to worse. The challenge is to listen to God, lean into the arms of love and begin to dance.

Fuel for your journey

1. Which story caused you to think of your own experiences? Why?

2. How does it make you feel?

3. What would you like to say to God right now?

4. Who can you share these feelings with?

CHAPTER TWELVE

Spirituality
Trusting in the Promise

Ezekiel, a prophet in the Old Testament, has seen a vision and he tells us his story. Let us listen to his experience.

"I, Ezekiel, have felt the powerful presence of the Lord and His spirit took me and sat me down in a valley where the ground was covered with bones. He led me all around the valley and I could see that there were very many bones. And they were very dry."

God asked, "Ezekiel, can these bones come back to life?"

"Sovereign Lord only you can answer that," Ezekiel replied.

"Prophesy to the bones," said God. "Tell these dry bones to listen to the word of the Lord. Tell them that I the Sovereign Lord am saying to them; I am going to put breath into you and bring you back to life. I will give you sinews and muscles and cover you with skin. Then you will know that I am the Lord."

So Ezekiel prophesied as God told him and while he was speaking he heard a rattling noise and the bones began to join together. While he watched, the bones were covered with sinew and muscles and then with skin. But there was no breath in the bodies.

God proclaimed, "Ezekiel prophesy to the wind. Tell the wind that the Sovereign Lord commands it to come from every direction to breathe into these dead bodies and bring them back to life."

So Ezekiel prophesied as he had been told. The wind began to blow from all directions. God's breath entered the bodies and they came to life and stood up.

"Ezekiel, my people are like these dry bones, they say that they are dried up without any hope and no future. So prophesy to these people and tell them that I the Sovereign Lord am going to open their graves. I am going to take them out and bring them back to me. When I open the graves where my people were buried and bring them out they will know that I am the Lord. I will put my breath in them, bring them back to life and they will live for me. Then they will know that I am the Lord. I have promised that I would do this—and I will. I the Lord have spoken."

"I, Ezekiel, in God's Name, tell you that He has given you new life. Join me in worshiping our Sovereign Lord."

And the people worshiped. "Holy, Holy, Holy is the Lord God Almighty, who was, who is and who is to come."

Ezekiel shouted, "As I watched the bones come to life, and dance their praise to our God, I felt His Spirit in the Wind and the power of it overcame me and I fell to my knees. Join me in worshiping our Sovereign Lord."

And the people worshiped, "Our Lord and God, you are worthy to receive glory, honor and power, for you have created all things and by your will they were given existence and life" (Ezekiel 37).

God promised Ezekiel the dry bones would be brought to life and God kept that promise. In the Holy Scriptures we discover numerous examples of God working in mysterious and miraculous ways to keep a promise. God has a destiny ordained for each of us. God makes the provision and it is our choice whether or not we want to take a step of faith believing the provision is for us. We will look at four stories of provisions made for those who were obedient and believed.

A Coincidence?

2 Kings 8:1-6,

> *Elisha once said to the woman whose son he had restored to life; "Get ready! Leave with your family and settle wherever you can, because the Lord has decreed a seven year famine which is coming to the land." The woman got ready and did as the man of God said, setting out with her family and settling in the land of the Philistines for seven years. At the end of the seven years, the woman returned from the land of the Philistines and went out to the king to claim her house and her field. The king was talking with Gehazi, the servant of the man of God. "Tell me," he said, "all the great things that Elisha has done." Just as he was relating to the king how his master had restored a dead person to life, the very woman whose son Elisha had restored to life came to the king to claim her house and field. "My lord king," Gehazi said, "this is the woman, and this is that son of hers whom Elisha restored to life." The king questioned the woman, and she*

*told him her story. With that the king placed
an official at her disposal, saying, "Restore all
her property to her, with all that the field produced from the day she left the land until
now."*

Was God's provision for this woman a coincidence or is there more to the story? Without understanding all the details or asking many questions of Elisha, the man of God, she chose to be obedient. She left the comforts and routine of home and went to a foreign land. She was among a people who did not have the same religious beliefs. It was in a strange setting that God provided for this woman and her son.

After seven years she returned to her homeland. God appointed that she would walk into a conversation with Elisha's servant, Gehazi, and the king. She had the opportunity to validate Elisha's ministry. God had saved her from famine in order to complete the work that He had planned for her to do. God used the relationship that had developed between Elisha and the woman to bring good to both of them. The woman was able to give a positive report for Elisha and God restored all the property and all the income the land had provided while she was gone.

God's Fuel

Have you ever stepped out into a strange situation only to find you received a blessing? Or has fear paralyzed your soul and limited your opportunities? Through this story God is asking us to trust Him in our times of famine and experience the joy of provision above and beyond even what we can imagine. Do you believe events disguised as a coincidence happen for a reason?

Defect Transformed into Treasure

Luke 19:1-10,

> *Jesus entered Jericho and was passing through. A man was there by the name of Zacchaeus; he was a chief tax collector and was wealthy. He wanted to see who Jesus was, but being a short man he could not, because of the crowd. So he ran ahead and climbed a sycamore fig tree to see him, since Jesus was coming that way.*
>
> *When Jesus reached the spot, he looked up and said to him, "Zacchaeus, come down immediately. I must stay at your house today." So he came down at once and welcomed him gladly.*
>
> *All the people saw this and began to mutter, "He has gone to be the guest of a sinner."*
>
> *But Zacchaeus stood up and said to the Lord, "Look, Lord! Here and now I give half my possessions to the poor, and if I have cheated anybody out of anything, I will pay back four times the amount."*
>
> *Jesus said to him, "Today salvation has come to this house, because this man, too, is a son of Abraham. For the Son of Man came to seek and to save what was lost."*

God planned even before Zacchaeus was born that a sycamore tree would be growing along the road for him to climb on that very day. The tree was provided for Zacchaeus, but he needed to be willing to climb the tree. He was short and may have seen his lack of stature as a defect. But, Zacchaeus was willing to do a most undignified thing for a tax collector. He climbed a tree so he could see Jesus. We are not told what he expected would happen when he saw Jesus. We believe

Zacchaeus had a hungry heart. So when Jesus invited Himself to Zacchaeus' house, He was welcomed immediately. Zacchaeus was ready for a change in his life. His heart was open and he was prepared to allow his decision to affect his life. Jesus built a relationship with Zacchaeus over dinner and trust was established between them. Jesus did not preach to Zacchaeus, because this man made the choice to do what his heart told him had to be done.

God's Fuel

Do you view a situation in your life as a defect? Do you believe it limits or hinders you from fulfilling your dream? God has a way of taking our defects and bringing forth beauty. Can you trust God with your defect and allow Him to transform it into a treasure? If you bring to God an open heart He will show you what needs to be done to receive new life.

Who do you think you are?

Matthew 20:20-23,

> *Then the mother of the sons of Zebedee approached him with her sons and did him homage, wishing to ask him for something. He said to her, "What do you wish?" She answered him; "Command that these two sons of mine sit, one at your right and the other at your left, in your kingdom." Jesus said in reply, "You do not know what you are asking. Can you drink the cup that I am going to drink?" They said to him, "We can." He replied, "My cup you will indeed drink, but to sit at my right and my left is not mine to give but is for those for whom it has been prepared by my Father."*

From other Scriptures it is believed that Salome may have been the mother of these sons. In her zeal, Salome got ahead of herself and was caught up in the situation. She wanted her sons to be recognized and receive a place of honor. She was thinking only of her own desires. Jesus replied with rather direct, rebuking words. He told her she did not know what she was asking. He turned these words around and said that instead of honor, His followers would be called to suffer. The words from Jesus did not deter Salome. She took them to heart and Scripture tells us that she was present at the crucifixion and resurrection. What may have seemed like a correction from Jesus was used by Salome to deepen her faith in Him. Her faith had caught fire and was strong enough to allow her to be present to Jesus as He went through His suffering.

God's Fuel

Does Jesus ask you like He did Salome, who do you think you are? Do you have a self-importance that is unacceptable in the kingdom of God? If strong words have been spoken to you, do not despair. In humbleness, move ahead with ears tuned to the Spirit of God. God is full of Grace just waiting to honor your obedience and openness. Sit and wait, allowing God to fill you with power and courage to live life with enthusiasm. You will become possessed by God rather than yourself.

Persistence is Rewarded

Matthew 15:21-28,

Then Jesus went from that place and withdrew to the region of Tyre and Sidon. And behold, a Canaanite woman of that district came and called out, "Have pity on me, Lord, Son of David! My daughter is tormented by a demon."

*But he did not say a word in answer to her. His
disciples came and asked him, "Send her away,
for she keeps calling out after us." He said in
reply, "I was sent only to the lost sheep of the
house of Israel." But the woman came and did
him homage, saying, "Lord, help me." He said in
reply, "It is not right to take the food of the children and throw it to the dogs." She said, "Please,
Lord, for even the dogs eat the scraps that fall
from the table of their masters." Then Jesus said
to her in reply, "O woman, great is your faith!
Let it be done for you as you wish." And her
daughter was healed from that hour.*

A Canaanite woman sought the attention of a Jewish
teacher. She had heard that Jesus could heal and cast out
demons. She realized that according to culture she had no
right to seek His help. She did not have the social status to
deserve a Jewish teacher's recognition. She broke down the
cultural barriers and pressed ahead at all costs. She believed if
Jesus could heal others there was no reason why He could not
heal her daughter. Jesus at first did not acknowledge her
request. The disciples even told Jesus she was a bother and
should be sent away. However, she was a woman with a mission and she was persistent. Nothing was going to stand in her
way. She believed Jesus could heal her daughter and no cost
was too great. Jesus wanted to know why she thought He
should heal her daughter. She came back with a reply and
stood her ground. She acknowledged that her nationality and
religious beliefs may be different than His, but that did not
mean He could not heal her daughter. Her faith was on fire
and she believed that with Jesus her daughter could experience
wholeness. Her persistence and faith produced healing for her
daughter.

God's Fuel

Do you feel that you are unworthy of God's attention? God's promises apply to others, but you do not qualify? Your prayers have hit a brick wall and you have received no response? God did not send Jesus into the world only for certain people. No, God loves all people and wants them to come to him with their needs. Sometimes we will be tested and need to remain persistent. But, do not lose heart, keep pressing on. Maybe God is asking you some hard questions and wants you to reach out in desperation for the help that only God is able to provide. God's promise is that He will never leave you nor forsake you and God keeps His word.

Fuel for your journey

1. What have you discovered about yourself after answering the questions in this chapter?

2. How do these discoveries make you feel?

3. How has God responded to your feelings?

4. Who can you share these feelings with?

CHAPTER THIRTEEN

Afterglow
Basking in the Glory

We see ourselves as common, ordinary clay pots, but God sees us very differently. God's vision, as we are refined through the fire, is to produce a community of people who are empowered by the Holy Spirit. The combination of each unique gift working together creates the impossible.

Creating such a community is like producing glass. The combination of the raw materials, which symbolize our strengths, weakness and past experiences, are mixed in the proper proportions, called the batch. Then God adds the fire of the Holy Spirit. The temperature of the fire depends on the composition of the mixture. The community is constantly changing as new members add their raw materials to the batch. The operation is continuous from the day the fire was first lit, the day of Pentecost, until the entire world is basking in the glory of God.

The Glory of God

*I saw that from what appeared to be his waist
up he looked like glowing metal, as if full of fire,
and that from there down he looked like fire;
and brilliant light surrounded him. Like the
appearance of a rainbow in the clouds on a
rainy day, so was the radiance around him. This
was the appearance of the likeness of the glory of
the Lord. When I saw it, I fell facedown, and I
heard the voice of one speaking.* Ezekiel 1:27-28

We have felt God speaking to us through creation as He did the morning we saw the clouds and the rainbow. We experienced a touch of God's glory as He revealed His truth to us. It was the awe of the glory that led us to praise and worship God. The fire was present in our spirits and this caused an explosion of faith. God used clouds resembling flames to draw our attention to the rainbow of truth bringing us healing.

God's Protective Presence

*And Elisha prayed, "O Lord, open his eyes so he
may see." Then the Lord opened the servant's
eyes, and he looked and saw the hills full of
horses and chariots of fire all around Elisha.*
2 Kings 6:17

When Lori had her final flashback she was at the REM conference. In the midst of the fear and pain she looked up and realized that people who cared were surrounding her. She felt safe and protected. The presence of the Holy Spirit working through others created a fire that burned the horror of her past and destroyed it.

God's Refining Fire

*I will refine them like silver and test them like
gold. They will call on my name and I will
answer them; I will say, "They are my people,"
and they will say, "The Lord is our God."*
Zechariah 13:9

Sara's refining process began with a well-meaning comment from a fellow church member, that if she removed her neck brace she would experience God's healing. She felt as if she has spent thirty years in the furnace dealing with the emotions that erupted about the question of her worthiness of God's healing touch. During that time, Sara's faith became refined like pure gold. Through experiencing God's glory, the truth was revealed that in God's presence the questions we carry in our hearts for so long are no longer important.

God's Righteous Anger

*See, the Lord is coming with fire, and his chari-
ots are like a whirlwind; He will bring down his
anger with fury, and his rebuke with flames of
fire.* Isaiah 66:15

Lori has learned that anger is not wrong; rather it is what we do with our anger. Being hit with a belt brought justified anger. God knows we are going to be angry about injustice both in our own life and in the world. How we express that anger is our choice. And with those choices come the consequences of God's fury.

God's Inspiring Word

*God's word is in my heart like a burning fire,
shut up in my bones. I am weary of holding it
in; indeed I cannot.* Jeremiah 20: 9

Since Sara was a teenager she has felt God's call upon her life. It burned within her although she didn't know how to give it expression. Some of her most intimate and meaningful spiritual experiences have brought forth the gift of speaking in tongues, her love language to God. What was burning within her has been given an expression. Through her conversations with God, her call has become focused and the burning within has taken on a new meaning.

God's Tools

"Is not my word like fire," declares the Lord, "and like a hammer that breaks the rock in pieces?" Jeremiah 23:29

Along Lori's journey of recovery she has realized that God was careful to reveal her memories piece by piece. In the beginning the memories were fragmented and blurry. As she worked through them she gained the strength to see a more complete picture. If the whole picture had been revealed, the rock of her past would have been too heavy to carry. Instead she has carried them piece by piece to God's altar and given them to Him.

God's Ever Present Fire

For the Lord your God is a consuming fire, a jealous God. Deuteronomy 4:24

Worshiping idols takes away from our time with God. Some of these idols are fear, shame, bitterness, anger, a judgmental spirit, self-pity or pride. When we allow these idols to consume our lives, God becomes jealous. We can choose to ask God for help in releasing our obsessions. He will provide a safe community for this to take place. In this environment we find love, hope and trust in the relationships that develop with God and others. This community is the fuel that creates divine energy, allowing its members to see the Glory of God.

God's Revelation

My heart grew hot within me, and as I medi-tated, the fire burned; then I spoke with my tongue. Psalm 39:3

Writing this book has brought an awareness of our need to set aside time to listen for God. Our patience has grown as we learned to watch and wait on God. It is often through the still small voice that we hear Him speak. Walking the labyrinth has guided us in our search for God. When we seek Him, He can be found. He is watching and waiting also and delights in our finding Him. The fire of His Spirit has grown hot within us and has burned within our souls and *Faith on Fire; Fueling Your Enthusiasm* has given us the opportunity to speak God's Truths.

The greatest revelation that we have received while writing is that we had chosen to make the hurts of the pasts our idols. They clouded our vision, deafened our ears and hardened our hearts. When the idols were destroyed, there was nothing left between God and us. Nothing except an amazing space of peace, joy and freedom, waiting to be filled with the love of God. We continue to be filled until we are overflowing with His goodness. As we spill over, the fire of the Holy Spirit is spread and ignited in others. Communities are created, truths are shared and the flames of *Faith on Fire* are growing. We will move forward, with complete trust in God's promise to always be with us.

And, our spirits dance…with enthusiasm.

Fuel for your journey to God

"Peace I leave with you; my peace I give you. I do not give to you as the world gives. Do not let your hearts be troubled and do not be afraid."
John 14:27

"And surely I will be with you always, to the very end of the age." Matthew 28:20b

Bibliography

Chapter 3:
Shame; A Faith Perspective by Robert H. Albers, PhD.
Published 1995 by The Haworth Press, Inc., New York

Chapter 4:
The Minister as Diagnostician by Paul W. Pruyser
Published in 1976 by Westminister Press, Philadelphia

Resources

Faith on Fire Web site:
www.faithonfireministry.com

Clinical Pastoral Education (C.P.E.):
www.acpe.org

Recovery of Hope:
www.philhaven.org

Moms In Touch:
www.momsintouch.org

Faith on Fire
Order Form

Postal orders: Faith on Fire
P.O. Box 217
St. Charles, Mi 48655

Website: www.faithonfireministry.com/buybooknow

Please send *Faith on Fire* to:

Name: _____

Address: _____

City: _____ State: _____

Zip: _____ Telephone: (_____) _____

Book Price: $14.95

Shipping: $3.00 for the first book and $1.00 for each additional book to cover shipping and handling within US, Canada, and Mexico. International orders add $6.00 for the first book and $2.00 for each additional book.

Or order from:
ACW Press
1200 HWY 231 South #273
Ozark, AL 36360

(800) 931-BOOK

or contact your local bookstore